BUSINESS/SCIENCE/TECHNOLOGY DIVISION
CHICAGO PUBLIC LIBRARY
400 SOUTH STATE STREET
CHICAGO, IL 60605

D1250938

DISCARD

NATURAL SCIENCES &
USEFUL ARTS DEPT.

THE CHICAGO PUBLIC LIBRARY

FORM 19

HOW TO OVERCOME YOUR FEAR OF FLYING

HOW TO OVERCOME
YOUR
FEAR OF FLYING

by Dr. Marvin L. Aronson

HAWTHORN BOOKS, INC.
Publishers
NEW YORK

616.852206
A267h

Cop. 2

HOW TO OVERCOME YOUR FEAR OF FLYING

Copyright © 1971 by Marvin L. Aronson. Copyright under International and Pan-American Copyright Conventions. All rights reserved, including the right to reproduce this book, or portions thereof, in any form, except for the inclusion of brief quotations in a review. All inquiries should be addressed to Hawthorn Books, Inc., 70 Fifth Avenue, New York, New York 10011. This book was manufactured in the United States of America and published simultaneously in Canada by Prentice-Hall of Canada, Limited, 1870 Birchmount Road, Scarborough, Ontario. Library of Congress Catalog Card Number: 76-158026.

1 2 3 4 5 6 7 8 9 10

DESIGN: Sam Green

THE CHICAGO PUBLIC LIBRARY

NOV 16 '71 B

R06007 16128

To Helen and Ruth

BUSINESS/SCIENCE/TECHNOLOGY DIVISION
CHICAGO PUBLIC LIBRARY
400 SOUTH STATE STREET
CHICAGO, IL 60605

Acknowledgments

I WISH TO EXPRESS my appreciation to David M. Aronson for his collaboration in researching and writing Chapter 3: "Realistic Aspects of Flying."

Grateful acknowledgment is made to the late Asya L. Kadis, formerly director of the Group Therapy Department at the Postgraduate Center for Mental Health, for her invaluable help and suggestions, and also to my friends and colleagues at the Postgraduate Center who helped me crystallize my thinking in how to apply special group methods to treating the phobic flyer.

I wish to thank the Air Transport Association of America for permission to quote extensively from its pamphlets "How Safe Is Flying?" and "How to Fly"; Grune & Stratton, Inc., and Lewis R. Wolberg, M.D., for permission to quote from Dr. Wolberg's *The Technique of Psychotherapy,* Volume II, pp. 820–822, 893–896, and 1295, 1967; the editor of *Psychotherapy* for permission to quote from "Behavioral Bibliotherapy: A Simple Home Remedy," Volume VII, 1970, pp. 118–119, by Drs. G. Donald Mac-Clean and Robert W. Graff.

Mr. Rouvim J. Feguine, of TWA, and Mr. S. H. Miller, of Pan Am, have been especially helpful to me in my efforts to learn more about commercial aviation. Thanks are also due to Mr. Karl Dahlem, of American Airlines, Mr. T. Ivan Pyle, of BOAC, Miss Joyce Martin, of Eastern Airlines, Mr. J. Peter Brunswick, of El Al, and Mr. Hans J. Rathke, of Lufthansa.

M. L. A.

vii

NATURAL HISTORY MUSEUM LIBRARY
CHICAGO PUBLIC LIBRARY
400 SOUTH STATE STREET
CHICAGO, ILLINOIS

Contents

Introduction:
How to Use This Book

My MAIN PURPOSE IN WRITING this book is to help you fly with a minimum of anxiety and a maximum of pleasure. Part I explains why people often are afraid to fly, and Part II suggests steps one can take to help overcome his fears. I recommend you read Part I first because lasting help depends on at least some understanding of the reasons for your fears.

Chapter 1 consists of a composite personality profile of fearful flyers who actively seek to overcome their fears. My guess is that you will find that these people are, in many ways, similar to yourself.

In Chapter 2 I delineate typical fears of apprehensive flyers. You will probably find at least some of your own fears mentioned. In working with apprehensive flyers I have been impressed with the repetitiveness of their fears. Many passengers seem to go through very similar experiences while traveling on modern commercial airliners.

In Chapter 3 I describe realistic aspects of commercial flying and consider such questions as "What makes a plane fly?" and "What steps do the airlines and federal government take to ensure your safety?" For those of you who have already flown, much of this material may be familiar. For others who have not yet taken the first step, this material will help to dispel simple fears of flying due to lack of information. If, after reading this chapter, you can fly without much anxiety, you really do not have a flying problem; most people experience *some* fear during flight.

Chapter 4 discusses the psychodynamics of phobias. I should tell you at this point that I regard all *incapacitating* (as opposed to mild or moderate) fears as fundamentally phobic in nature. The more you understand how phobias work, the better you will be able to deal with your specific fears of flying. Also, this knowledge may help you cope with other phobic tendencies in yourself. Chapter 5 deals specifically with the flying phobia and discusses the symbolic meaning of flying. It explains why this pleasurable experience so often becomes charged with pain and fear and offers clinical examples of dreams, fantasies and drawings of fearful flyers with whom I have worked.

In Chapter 6 I outline practical steps you can take to overcome the fear of flying. The steps suggested do not require "deep" insight into the nature of your flying fears, nor do they require professional help. Some of you will be able to fly after reading this material and following the suggestions offered.

If these steps do not enable you to fly, read Chapter 7, which describes how to overcome fears by availing yourself of professional help. This professional help does not necessitate long-term psychotherapy. In recent years therapists have developed many effective methods by means of which they can aid people with phobias much more quickly—frequently, in one to fifteen sessions. In Chapter 8 I describe how to use special group methods to overcome fears of flying. The methods outlined can be adapted by you and others, provided professional therapists are available in your area. At the conclusion of the book I include a list of selected references, should you want to read further on commercial aviation or psychological matters related to the fear of flying.

PART I

Who Seeks Help
for the Fear of Flying?

RECENTLY THE BEHAVIOR SCIENCE Corporation of California interviewed 1,600 individuals from all parts of the United States on attitudes toward flying. Twenty-five percent of this sample turned out to be non-flyers, although all could afford to fly. The typical non-flyer, or "psychocentric" individual, according to this study, "is someone who is bound up by his own feelings of inadequacies or failures in life. He worries about the smaller events, and this affects him to the point where he does not have energy left to meet the more important daily challenges. In general, he is a follower, not a leader, and his life tends to be bound up in a more restricted personal and geographic space." [1] According to these researchers "psychocentric" individuals tend to be "territory-bounded." [2] Many of them do not feel much of a need to see new places. If they travel at all, they do not travel often, nor do they go very far by plane or by any means of transportation. In addition, they suffer from "generalized anxieties" and "spend most of their lives in a state of anxiety fretting about everything, even when they can't point to any specific problem. They feel powerless to control their own lives. They are helpless in the hands of fate."

"Flying types," by contrast, are venturesome. They go

[1] Curt Schleier, "A Campaign Against Fear," *Air Travel,* May, 1970, p. A18.
[2] Advertisement entitled, "Should the Airlines Write You Off as Hopeless?" *Reader's Digest,* May, 1970.

places and do things that other people only "hope to do someday." Not that they have more time or money, but they enjoy new experiences and are willing to invest time and money in them. Also "They are self-confident. They feel comfortable with themselves, are sure of their own capabilities and have trust in themselves as people." Finally, "they are involved and interested in the world around them." They involve themselves with other people in other places and exhibit an enthusiastic interest in whatever they do.[3]

The "psychocentric" person rarely seeks help for fears of flying. He is typically so bogged down by the routines of everyday living that it does not even occur to him to travel to distant places or to compete for the kind of high-echelon position that requires flying. Basically he avoids anxiety by suppressing his need to fly. On the other hand the person who is motivated enough to obtain professional help to overcome his fears cannot accept this solution. He feels he must fly and will not settle for less.

On the whole, the people who come to me with fears of flying are exceptionally well functioning. They are far above the national average in intelligence, education and achievement. The bulk of them are college graduates; a large proportion have had graduate or professional training. They are usually over thirty. Sociologically, they would be classified as upper middle class. Typically, the men are executives in such fields as advertising and publishing, owners of business firms or professionals: physicians, lawyers, dentists, college professors, accountants, journalists, and commercial photographers. The women are artists, writers, decorators, models, actresses or housewives, married to the type of man just described.[4]

[3] *Ibid.*

[4] Colleagues of mine at the Postgraduate Center for Mental Health in New York City report that these personality and socioeconomic patterns are consistent with their findings. I suspect that the picture would be essentially the same in other parts of the United States as well.

In addition these people are perfectionists. They demand a lot of themselves at work and in play. They are also action-oriented. They want to do many things and do them well. They want to see as much of the world as possible. They are afraid of becoming "obsolescent" as it becomes increasingly difficult to travel long distances by ship or rail. Needless to say, they feel terribly embarrassed at having a disabling symptom that seems to them so incongruous with their usual self-image. Some are aware of having other problems (and have even had psychotherapy for these). Others regard fear of flying as their *sole* symptom —their Achilles' heel.

Many are emotionally convinced that their next flight will be their last. Although they often do not expect anything unfortunate to happen to other members of their family while flying, they are sure their *own* luck will run out. Quoting safety statistics to them is useless.[5] They know plane travel is safe, but they remain convinced that it is dangerous for *them* to fly.

Women who are afraid to fly usually accept much more readily than men the idea that their fears spring from psychological causes. Consequently they are not as preoccupied with safety statistics, technological aspects of aviation, and the like. Their anxiety is much closer to the surface, and they are more afraid of becoming openly "hysterical" on a plane. (Men are also fearful of being embarrassed during flights but have more confidence in their ability to control the overt expression of their feelings.) Finally, women are more concerned with the effects of their flying on children and other family members.

In summary, the people who seek help for the fear of

[5] Even the following quotation from the February 26, 1971, issue of *Life* fails to make a dent in their fears: "1970 was the safest year for U.S. scheduled airlines since the commercial jet age began in the late 1950s. In fact, it was close to perfect. Two travelers killed in the last week of December in a St. Thomas, Virgin Islands, crash were the only air fatalities on U.S. scheduled flights in all of 1970."

flying are considerably above average in intelligence and achievement. They are extremely distressed because they cannot fly. They are unwilling to "accept" their symptom. They are strongly motivated to overcome it. In most respects they are exceptionally rational. However, in talking about their fears of flying they seem to abdicate their capacity for logical thinking. They become inordinately dependent on the therapist *in this one area.*

You are probably asking yourself, "How are these people different from other well-functioning people who are *not* afraid to fly?" The answer is that they have unconsciously attached pre-existing anxieties to the concept of flight. The mechanisms by which this takes place will be discussed at length in Chapter 4 ("What Is a Phobia?") and Chapter 5 ("The Flying Phobia").

At this point I would simply like to state that if your fear of flying developed recently and was specifically activated by an actual air accident, you will find it much easier to overcome than if you have been afraid for many years or developed the fear in the absence of any observable precipitating event.

In the Introduction I predicted that you would share certain personality characteristics of the typical fearful flyer who seeks professional help for this problem. It might be interesting for you to compare your personality patterns with those of the flyers just described and see to what extent my prediction was correct.

CHAPTER 2

What Fearful Flyers
Say They Fear

IF YOU ASKED THE AVERAGE person what frightened him most about taking a flight, he would answer, "I am afraid the plane might crash and I would die." Many fearful flyers, by contrast, are unable to say exactly what they fear. They know they are afraid but cannot describe their fears in words. An even larger number express fears that have no logical relationship to the idea of a plane crash or death.

I would like to present, in this chapter, a sample of the prior to flight, on the way to the airport, on the plane, and frightening thoughts that occur to fearful flyers in the weeks at their destination. I will not, at this point, discuss the psychological reasons for these fears. These will become clearer to you in Chapter 5, "The Flying Phobia." The chances are that at least some of your conscious fears will appear in the following lists. It is, however, possible that your specific fears may be so idiosyncratic that they have not occurred to other flyers. The more imaginative you are the greater the likelihood you will have fears that nobody has ever thought of before. Intelligence is of little help in forestalling irrational fears of flying.

TYPICAL FEARS *BEFORE* A FLIGHT
Will not know what clothes to pack
Will not have chosen the right travel agent
Will not know which airline to take
Will not know what type of plane to take

Will not be able to decide whether to take a night or a day flight

Will not be able to decide whether to take a direct flight or a stopover

Will not be able to decide whether to fly with a spouse or alone

Will not be able to get affairs in order in time

Will not be able to obtain passport in time

Will not have paid rent or mortgage on time

Will not have completed one's will

Will not have enough money for trip

Will not have forgotten to turn off the gas, water, or electricity at home

Will miss important mail while on trip

Will not be able to leave because of illness of self or family members

Will not be able to leave because of a family crisis or emergency

Will not get to airport on time

Will not be able to obtain a taxi to the airport

Will get a flat tire on the way to the airport

Will be delayed by an airline strike

Will not be able to find departure building

Will be unable to take off due to mechanical difficulties, bad weather, etc.

Will be able to obtain insurance at the airport—a bad omen signifying plane will crash

Will be *unable* to obtain insurance at airport

Will lose luggage

Will find out luggage is overweight

Will have forgotten airplane tickets

Will find out that plane has been overbooked

Will be unable to sit next to spouse, friends or family

Will not hear flight announcement at airport and consequently will miss plane

Will not be able to obtain a drink before entering plane

Will forget to take along necessary medication or tranquilizers

Many of the above fears, you will note, are no different from fears people have prior to embarking on any trip. They all boil down to a fear that something will prevent the traveler from reaching his destination easily and safely.

TYPICAL FEARS *DURING* A FLIGHT

Fear of fainting in boarding area
Fear of tripping on boarding ramp
Fear of being sucked into jet engine
Fear of sitting in front of plane
Fear of sitting in middle of plane
Fear of sitting in rear of plane
Fear of plane being too empty
Fear of plane being too crowded
Fear of being dressed improperly (especially women)
Fear of not "fitting in" with other passengers
Fear that other passengers will not be "one's type"
Fear of not liking other passengers
Fear of having to look out of window
Fear of not being able to see wing through window
Fear of being sucked through window
Fear of feeling a compulsion to walk in aisle
Fear of *not* being able to walk in aisle
Fear that walking in aisle will "rock the plane too much"
Fear of sitting too close to family members
Fear of not being able to sit close enough to family members
Fear of not being close enough to emergency exits
Fear of being *too* close to emergency exits (and being swept through)
Fear of being trapped between two adjacent passengers
Fear that adjacent passenger will be too nervous
Fear that adjacent passenger will be too calm
Fear that adjacent passenger will be hostile, indifferent or humiliating
Fear that adjacent passenger will notice one's panic
Fear that adjacent passenger will become panicky or violent
Fear of discomforting adjacent passenger

Fear of angering adjacent passenger

Fear of not being able to hear public-address system

Fear of misunderstanding public-address announcements

Fear that captain and crew will omit important flight information regarding weather, altitude, speed, arrival time, etc.

Fear that captain and crew will not inform one of danger

Fear that captain's announcements are really a subterfuge to conceal danger

Fear that captain and crew will disclose unnecessary frightening information

Fear that the captain may have had a fight with his wife and will be unable to fly properly

Fear that captain may be inebriated

Fear that captain is incompetent

Fear that captain will get a heart attack or otherwise become incapacitated

Fear that captain and co-pilot will be at odds with each other, endangering flight

Fear of not being able to understand stewardess' instructions on use of oxygen masks

Fear that stewardess' instructions on life preserver portend crash over water

Fear of being snubbed by stewardess

Fear of being laughed at or criticized by stewardess

Fear that stewardess will be unable to help in emergency

Fear that stewardess will be unwilling to help in emergency

Fear that stewardess will not serve meal on time

Fear that stewardess will not serve liquor on time

Fear of being unable to get to restroom

Fear of being locked in restroom

Fear of becoming ill in restroom

Fear of not being able to urinate or defecate in restroom

Fear of hitting one's head against ceiling of restroom

Fear of falling through toilet (in case of children)

Fear of being unable to return to one's seat

Fear of vomiting

Fear of becoming "hysterical"
Fear of acting "crazy"
Fear of "running amok"
Fear of screaming
Fear of an appendicitis attack
Fear of a heart attack
Fear of ear drums bursting
Fear of an explosion
Fear of a sudden fire
Fear of a "mad bomber"
Fear of hijacking
Fear of sabotage
Fear of "bells ringing" or other sounds
Fear of changes in engine sounds
Fear of strange odors on plane
Fear that plane is flying too low
Fear that plane is flying too high
Fear that plane is flying too slowly
Fear that plane is flying too fast
Fear that pressurization system is not working properly
Fear that window will burst open
Fear that life preserver will not inflate
Fear that wings will snap off
Fear that plane has insufficient fuel
Fear that plane will turn over on its side during banking
   maneuvers
Fear that plane will break in two
Fear that plane will develop a hole in its bottom
Fear that plane will "run out of gas"
Fear that plane will be struck by lightning
Fear that thunder will damage plane
Fear that plane will crash into flying birds
Fear that plane will crash into mountain
Fear that plane will crash into water
Fear that plane will crash into other planes in vicinity of
   airport
Fear that plane will miss runway
Fear that plane will overshoot runway

Fear that landing equipment will not work
Fear that "one's number" is up
Fear that this will be one's last flight

TYPICAL FEARS AT DESTINATION

Fear of losing one's baggage at airport
Fear of being delayed or arrested at customs
Fear of being unable to get a taxi to hotel
Fear that hotel reservations will not be honored
Fear that hotel personnel will not understand English
Fear of elevators in hotel
Fear of becoming ill or dying in hotel room
Fear of being alone in a desolate hotel room
Fear of developing claustrophobia in hotel room
Fear of insects or germs in hotel room
Fear of strange noises in hotel room
Fear of food poisoning in restaurants
Fear of getting lost
Fear of walking alone on streets
Fear of walking in large open spaces
Fear of crossing bridges
Fear of climbing mountains
Fear of mob violence
Fear of political revolution
Fear of being attacked by cats, dogs, snakes, or other animals
Fear of not having sufficient time to pack prior to next flight
Fear of not being able to consummate one's business deal successfully (if this is a business trip)
Fear of something happening to children back home
Fear of becoming too frightened to go to the next stop or to return home
Fear that one's luck will run out on this trip
Fear that return trip will prove fatal

Some of the fears that occur to passengers aboard

planes may be due to lack of information about flying, particularly if the flyer has never flown before or is unfamiliar with new developments in commercial flight. I believe the airlines could render a valuable service to fearful flyers by distributing an anonymous checklist of realistic fears to passengers prior to take-off and having the captain deal with these in the course of his public-address announcements.[1]

Some of the airlines now provide a Flight Service Director on the Boeing 747 to answer passengers' questions and to put them at ease. This service is an excellent way of dispelling fears due to lack of information. Also the "personal touch" can be tremendously reassuring. It would be especially helpful to fearful flyers if they could speak briefly with, or at least catch a glimpse of, the captain or co-pilot prior to take-off.

It should be obvious, however, that most of the fears listed in this chapter have little or nothing to do with objective facts. Any attempt to dispel these by realistic explanations would be useless, since they reflect inner turmoil and have little to do with the realities of flight.

In Chapters 4 and 5 I will attempt to explain the psychological significance of these fears. In Chapters 6 and 7 I will indicate how some of them can be desensitized or otherwise ameliorated. In the meantime, see if you can determine which of these fears correspond to your own. Pay particularly close attention to those that cause you to hold your breath or make your pulse beat faster. Do not become discouraged if you have difficulty in describing your fears explicitly at this point. They will occur to you as you read on. Eventually, if you have not already done so, you will come to realize that these fears are symptomatic of more basic anxieties that have become attached to flying.

[1] For other recommendations on how to dispel passenger fears, see Robert J. Serling, *Loud and Clear* (New York: Dell, 1970), pp. 26–38.

CHAPTER 3

Realistic Aspects
of Flying

IN THIS CHAPTER I would like to provide you with information on realistic aspects of flying with the aim of showing you that commercial aviation is safer than most people realize. If you have already flown, much of this information may be familiar. However, if you have never flown, this material may help allay fears due primarily to lack of information.

Unfortunately, most people know far too little about aviation. It is still possible to go through many years of schooling without learning even the rudiments of aviation. This is less true of the younger generation and probably accounts in part for the fact that fear of flying is a rarity among youthful passengers.

The chapter is divided into five sections: 1) "What Makes an Airplane Fly?," 2) "Description of a Typical Flight," 3) "The Airline Industry in the United States" (including a discussion of airplane manufacturing, airline operations, and pilot and stewardess training), 4) "The Role of the Government in Modern Commercial Aviation," and 5) "Air Safety."

I would suggest you read carefully those sections which bear on your fears. The others may be skipped over lightly.

WHAT MAKES AN AIRPLANE FLY?

An understanding of some of the properties of air will help you to grasp the essentials of flight. Although we cannot see air, it has weight and when in motion can exert force. Here are two simple demonstrations of the power of air to move objects:

1. Place a piece of paper vertically against the palm of your hand and blow against it. The paper will remain suspended as long as you continue to blow.

2. Hold a large sheet of paper in your hand. It will hang down as long as you stand still, but if you run with it the paper will be pushed upward. It will "fly" parallel to the ground.[1]

In order for a plane to fly it must overcome gravity and drag (air resistance). It must have sufficient *lift* and *thrust*. *Lift* offsets gravity; *thrust* offsets drag. The upward push of *lift* is provided by the dynamic action of air against a plane's wings. The forward push of *thrust* is provided by its jet engines.

Bernoulli's Principle states that the pressure of a gas (including air) decreases as the speed of the gas increases. The consequences of this for flight are as follows: (1) Faster-moving air along the upper surface of the wing creates a low-pressure area. (2) Since gases always move from a high-pressure area to a low-pressure area, the air below the plane's wing moves upward into the low-pressure area. (3) This exerts force on the wing and lifts it upward.

To demonstrate how air moving from a lower to a higher pressure area can push an object upward, try the following experiment: Curve a small card slightly and bend one end around a pencil. Blow across the top of the card. The card will rise toward the air stream because the air you blow across the top of the card has a lower air pressure than the air which pushes against the under-surface of the card.[2]

Lift can be increased by speeding the flow of air over

[1] These and other simple aerodynamic experiments are described in *The World Book Encyclopedia* (Chicago: Field, 1962), I, 77.
[2] *Ibid.*

the top of the wing. One way to gain more lift is to increase the plane's air speed. The faster the air speed, the greater the difference in air pressure above and below the wings. "Lift increases approximately with the square of the air speed. For example, doubling the air speed increases the lift four times." [3] Another way to gain more lift is by increasing the wing's "angle of attack" to the oncoming air flow. This makes the distance over the top of the wing longer. Air traveling over the top of the wing has to travel faster, causing the air pressure in that area to drop. The air below the wing rises and causes it to lift.

Basically, the function of a jet engine is to achieve sufficient *thrust* to propel the plane forward against the retarding forces of drag. Once a plane reaches its cruising speed, less thrust is necessary because the plane has a tendency to continue on its forward path through inertia. Jet engines achieve their thrust by accelerating a mass of gas to the rear of the plane. This produces a counter-thrust that moves the plane forward. The scientific principle underlying this phenomenon is Newton's Third Law of Motion: Every action produces an equal and opposite reaction. To demonstrate this law, observe the action of an inflated balloon when air is suddenly released from it. The balloon will be propelled forward by the rush of escaping air and will continue to "fly" until the compressed air escapes. [4]

A jet engine works as follows: Air enters into the front end of the engine, where it is compressed to more than five times normal pressure. This compressed air is then forced rearward into a combustion chamber. Here fuel, usually refined kerosene, is sprayed with the air and ignited. The mixture of high-pressure air and fuel burns at very high temperatures. Continual explosions of air and fuel produce gushes of hot expanding gases, which, as they escape from the rear of the engine at speeds of more than 1,200 miles per hour, propel the airplane forward.

[3] *Ibid.,* p. 74.
[4] *Ibid.,* p. 77.

The escaping gases also turn a turbine that provides continual power for the compressors.[5]

The attitude and motion of a plane during flight are controlled by manipulating movable surfaces on its wing and tail. The "elevator" (the control surface on the horizontal part of the tail) controls the up-and-down movement of the plane in pitch. The "rudder" (the control surface on the vertical part of the tail) controls the sideway movement of the plane in yaw. In addition, immovable parts of the tail help keep the airplane stable. (The horizontal, fixed-tail part is called the stabilizer; the vertical surface is called the fin.) "Ailerons" are movable parts on the trailing edge of the wings which control the plane in roll. The pilot usually operates the elevator, rudder, and ailerons together. He uses the rudder and the ailerons to "bank" or roll the airplane during turns. He uses the elevator to point the nose of the plane upward to increase the "angle of attack." [6]

DESCRIPTION OF A TYPICAL FLIGHT [7]

Most airplane passengers are unaware of the extensive pre-flight planning and preparations which routinely precede every flight. Before passengers enter an airplane, skilled airline maintenance teams service each of its systems. They check the many instruments aboard to make sure that all equipment is in top working order. They clean and sanitize its interior. Under the careful supervision of the flight engineer they pump fuel into the large tanks connected to the jet engines. The flight engineer makes sure that the proper amount of fuel goes to each

[5] For further information on the operation of jet engines see James T. Bernardo, *Aviation and Space in the Modern World* (rev. ed.; New York: E. P. Dutton, 1968).

[6] *The World Book Encyclopedia*, p. 78.

[7] The material in this section is based largely on John Bainbridge, *Like a Homesick Angel* (Boston: Houghton Mifflin, 1964).

tank in the correct sequence. The Federal Aviation Administration requires that every airplane carry sufficient fuel to 1) reach its destination, 2) fly in holding patterns for thirty minutes, and 3) reach a designated alternate airport.[8]

After the maintenance crews finish their preparations, the flight engineer makes a detailed check of the aircraft. First he examines the "engine log," a record of all past flights made by the airplane. Then he studies reports of engine performance, making sure that even slight malfunctions have been repaired. If he notices anything unusual, he consults with the foreman of the company's maintenance department. Next he makes a meticulous inspection of the outside of the airplane. Walking in a complete circle, he checks the conditions of the nose, wings, engines, tail and landing equipment. He looks for weak spots in the structural metal that covers the aircraft. Following this external inspection, he performs a detailed examination of the interior of the airplane.

Meanwhile, airline route planners devise a "flight plan." Prior to take-off, airline weathermen and flight dispatchers map out the most efficient path for the jet liner on the basis of the latest U.S. Weather Bureau forecasts. This is called the "minimum time route." Two or more alternate routes are also prepared as precautions against rapid changes in weather conditions.

The flight plan contains precise figures on such items as the take-off weight of fuel loaded, rate of fuel consumption, and amount of fuel reserve carried. It lists the precise times that the aircraft will pass over each radio-reporting ground station. Latest weather forecasts are provided for destination airports as well as for several alternate landing destinations.

On overseas flights the captain, first officer, and flight engineer meet at the airline's briefing or flight dispatch

[8] Robert Lindsey, *The New York Times,* July 7, 1970.

offices as early as two hours before scheduled departure. Here the captain critically reviews the flight plan and consults with his crew and the dispatcher. He may alter the planned route or altitudes if he feels it desirable. He relies on weather charts, which are constantly revised as new information is received. (U.S. Weather Bureau meteorologists obtain data from the weather balloons sent up from the mainland as well as from weather ships; they also receive direct weather reports from aircraft en route over the ocean.) [9]

Wind conditions are especially important in planning a minimum time route on overseas flights. Because there is less air-traffic congestion over the ocean, captains may have a choice of up to five or six "tracks" (flight paths). Route planning allows them to take advantage of helpful winds while avoiding delaying cross-winds.

In route planning for domestic flights, the choice of alternate paths is limited by the tremendous volume of air traffic. The captain has to fly in the specific air corridor assigned to him by FAA flight controllers. This restrictive procedure ensures that regardless of the amount of air traffic, each aircraft will be flying in a recognized zone. FAA regulations require that each plane be protected on all sides by sufficient air space.

Recently, computers have been developed that greatly facilitate the preparation of flight plans. A computer can devise a transatlantic flight plan in about one minute. It utilizes stored information, including the number of flight paths and their distances on the North Atlantic route map, technical data for the type of aircraft being used, and the mathematical formulas necessary to calculate times, course, fuel, weight, etc. The dispatcher analyzes the alternate tracks worked out by the computer. He uses a series of "operational criteria" to select the best route. These are (1) higher flight safety, (2) improved passenger comfort

[9] Lufthansa, *Technical Bulletin,* January 31, 1969, p. 2.

(avoidance of bad weather), (3) greater punctuality and (4) increased economy.[10]

When the captain is completely satisfied with the flight plan, he signs it and files it with air traffic control. The captain of an overseas flight usually boards his plane a full thirty minutes before the scheduled departure time. On short domestic flights, where less planning is necessary, he arrives about fifteen minutes prior to departure.

The pilot (captain) and co-pilot (first officer) sit facing identical instrument panels. The fail-safe design of commercial airliners provides every important system with one or more alternate back-up systems which can function perfectly if the original fails. The complicated computers and sensitive navigational instruments used for automatic flying (instrument flight) are duplicated and, in some instances, even triplicated. The captain and the first officer are the human links in the airplane's elaborate safety back-up systems. They man the same controls, watch the same indicators and hear the same communications. In case of an emergency the captain, first officer or flight engineer are all capable of flying the airplane individually.

Before joining the captain and first officer in the cockpit, the flight engineer makes a final check of the interior of the airplane. He makes sure that all safety equipment is in top working order. "Safety gear on one modern jetliner (hatches, fuel dumping installations, fire detection and extinguishing systems, duplicate instruments, emergency brakes, emergency evacuation lighting, et cetera) weighs approximately as much as 15 passengers and their baggage." [11]

The last phase of preparation for a flight occurs inside the cockpit. The captain and first officer sit forward in the cockpit, peer through slanted windows, and face identical instrument panels. The captain sits on the left, the first

[10] *Ibid.,* pp. 5–7.
[11] Stuart G. Tipton, "How Safe Is Flying?" (Washington, D.C.: Air Transport Association of America pamphlet, 1970), p. 13.

officer on the right. The flight engineer's seat is behind the first officer's, on a slightly higher level. His desk and several instrument panels (for the aircraft's various systems) face to the right. During the final minutes before take-off the pilot (captain) and his co-pilot (first officer) systematically follow an elaborate checklist. One at a time, and in correct sequence, hundreds of items are checked to ensure that all controls and instruments are working properly.

If his plane is overweight when it reaches the runway, the captain may burn extra fuel by taxiing very slowly from the boarding ramp to the runway. If necessary, he can burn additional excess fuel at the runway by pushing up the throttles while keeping the brakes on.

"Airliners have demonstrated that they are capable of carrying far heavier loads than their regular capacity. A DC-4 was once accidentally loaded twice and flew with six extra tons of cargo. A jet liner engaged in emergency evacuation airlifted 303 passengers—almost twice its capacity." [12]

The most important rule in successfully flying jets is to "fly by the book"—that is, strictly according to the information worked out by electronic computers. Before take-off the captain knows exactly how many feet of runway his airplane will require in relation to its weight and existing barometric pressure. Even the slightest variation from standard conditions many pose a serious threat to the safe operation of the aircraft. For instance, if the temperature increases one degree, a 707 needs an additional fifty feet of runway. If the barometric pressure drops one tenth of an inch, another hundred feet of runway is necessary. To ensure that all conditions prescribed by the airplane's computers are met, the captain checks informational lights, gauges and dials on his instrument panel. "Take nothing for granted" is the guiding principle for

[12] *Ibid.*, p. 16.

commercial-airline pilots. Air safety is not an accident. It is the consequence of careful preparation and constant checking.

Following is a description of a typical flight of a Boeing 707 flying from New York to Paris.[13] The Boeing 707, a "work horse" four-engine jet used by many airlines on longer flights, seats upwards of 150 passengers (each airline has its own seating arrangements) and measures 152 feet, 11 inches in length—more than half as long as a football field. Its cockpit contains 340 switches, 437 circuit breakers, 150 warning lights, and dozens of dials, levers and gauges. Most of the radio and electronic equipment is packed away under the flight deck to give the cockpit a trimmer appearance, but it may be easily reached during the flight if adjustments become necessary.

Passengers fasten their seat belts for take-off. The seat in a modern jet is quite safe. It is "built to withstand nine times the force of gravity, which means it would take nine times the weight of a 170-pound man to tear it loose." [14] The area each seat occupies is standardized by international agreement. The stewardesses demonstrate how to use the oxygen masks provided for all crew members and passengers. These masks drop down automatically from storage compartments in the ceiling of the cabin in the unlikely event that the airplane loses its pressurization. Loss of cabin pressure is unlikely because the windows in a jet are made of two layers of glass with a clear layer of plastic between. They can bulge six to eight inches without blowing out. If the cabin did lose pressure, the captain could make an emergency descent (in about one minute) to altitudes where the outside air is breathable. In the cockpit the first officer calls off a series of forty-five

[13] The description of this flight is based largely on Bainbridge. Similar descriptions may be found in Barry J. Schiff, *The Boeing 707* (New York: Arco, 1967), and Robert J. Serling, *Loud and Clear* (New York: Dell, 1970).

[14] Tipton, p. 12.

"commands" from a checklist entitled "Before Starting Engines." The captain replies to these commands. Then the first officer reads a section of the checklist consisting of twenty-seven items. These are answered by the flight engineer.

After the engines are started the captain usually speaks to the passengers over the public-address system, giving a preview of the flight. When he finishes his talk the captain and first officer turn to the section of the checklist headed "After Starting Engines" and complete the thirteen items in that section. By now the captain has been notified by the airport control tower which runway he can use. The assigned runway for this flight is 14,600 feet—approximately 5,000 feet longer than the minimum required by law for the 707. The captain then grasps a control called the "nose-wheel steering device." This control, attached to the side of the cockpit, resembles one third of an automobile steering wheel. The captain releases the brakes and the airplane moves slowly away from the terminal. While taxiing, seven items in the "Taxi—Before Take-off" portion of the checklist are called out.

After the captain receives permission to take off from the airport control tower, he follows the nine commands in the "When Cleared for Take-off" section of the check-list. Then, with the brakes set, he scrutinizes five sets of gauges located in the center of his instrument panel. These give him information about the exhaust temperature, the second turbine, and the fuel flow of all four engines. Take-off is attempted only if all these gauges give satisfactory readings.

The first officer pushes the starting button of his instrument panel's stop clock and calls out, "Time!" The captain releases the brakes and the 150-ton plane begins to move. The captain guides the 707 by means of the nose-wheel steering device. The first officer holds the "yoke," a control which looks like "a fat black steering wheel" cut in half. The yoke controls the "elevator"—a movable part on the tail of the airplane. During the initial phase of take-off it is held forward to keep direct contact between the airplane and the ground. For the first twenty seconds of take-off the 707 builds slowly to a speed of about seventy miles per hour. Then the captain opens the throttles slightly and the jet engines respond with a high-pitched wail. Twenty-five seconds into take-off, the airplane travels ninety-three miles per hour and quickly builds up momentum for take-off. The captain grasps the yoke, moving it back slightly. At this point he controls the airplane by means of its rudder and ailerons.

Forty-two seconds into take-off the 707 reaches a speed of 138 miles per hour. Since this is the proper acceleration speed for this particular flight, the first officer indicates his approval by calling out "Time O.K.!" If the airplane had not reached its designated speed after forty-two seconds, the first officer would have called out, "Abort!" and the captain would have stopped the take-off. He still has more than 9,000 feet of runway in which to stop the airplane by pulling back the throttles, reversing the engines and applying the brakes.

Forty-seven seconds into take-off the jet attains a speed of 170 miles per hour. After this critical point, called "V-One," is reached, the take-off can no longer be aborted. Four seconds later, the first officer calls out, "V-R!" indicating that the plane has reached the velocity at which it should be pointed up. The captain pulls back on the yoke. The jet stays on the runway for three seconds more, building its speed to 285 feet per second (193 mph). The first officer calls out, "V-Two!" and the plane, now pointing upward, begins to rise.

The captain retracts the landing gear as soon as the airplane is a few feet above the runway. He points the airplane upward at an angle of about seven degrees. The airplane is now climbing at a speed of 215 miles per hour.

Because noise-pollution levels near airports are so high, some planes temporarily reduce the roar of their jet engines during take-off. The noise-abatement procedure on this flight occurs fourteen seconds after leaving the runway. After lowering the power about one third and then flying level for a minute, the captain points the airplane up again. As it continues to climb, the "After Take-off" section of the checklist, consisting of eleven items, is called off. By now the airplane is traveling at about 400 miles per hour.

The captain checks with air traffic control stations to make sure that the cruising altitude he has requested for the transatlantic crossing is still available. (Cruising heights for modern jet liners range from 25,000 feet to 43,000 feet. The optimal height is about 33,000 feet.) After reaching the airplane's assigned cruising altitude the captain usually takes a short break to stretch his legs. The plane now flies at a cruising speed close to 600 miles per hour.

There is less vibration on jet flights than on most buses, cars and trains. This quiet ride is the result of specially designed sound-suppression systems which cost an average of $25,000. Airlines often provide entertainment, such as movies and pre-recorded music, on longer flights. To provide these "extras," a modern jet has an electrical system that could serve the needs of 150 average-size homes.[15] Refreshments, snacks or complete meals (depending on the time of day) are served to passengers on virtually all domestic and international flights. Alcoholic beverages are offered for purchase on all flights.

Occasionally jet airliners encounter turbulence—bumpy air usually found in cloud areas. Although turbulence may be unpleasant, it rarely poses a safety threat to modern jets, which have been constructed to withstand much greater stresses. The wings on a 707 are swept back at an angle of thirty-five degrees and move up and down in an arc that may reach eighteen feet at the tips.

Bad weather conditions no longer pose serious hazards

[15] *Ibid.,* p. 14.

on commercial flights, because jets fly *over* the weather about 95 percent of the time and are additionally equipped with radar search systems which steer the plane away from storm areas up to 150 miles away. Weather is important primarily during take-off and landing. Since fog, cross-winds, low clouds, rising sand and heavy rains or snow may close airports, a generally accepted safety rule is that a plane should have suitable landing weather conditions at its destination and at one alternate airport before it receives permission to take off.

The problem of "icing" (ice sticking to wings or in the engines) does not normally affect jets, since they fly considerably above the highest level at which water freezes into ice (20,000 feet). If icing difficulties occur while the airliner is climbing to, or descending from, its cruising altitude, ice-warning lights trigger de-icing and anti-icing systems on all vulnerable sections of the aircraft.

Winds do not have much effect upon commercial airliners because wind speed (50–100 mph) is trivial in comparison to the cruising speed of jets (600 mph). Tail winds or oncoming winds alter the length of jet flight by only a few minutes.

Modern navigational equipment, including complex radio and radar units, has practically eliminated the possibility of a jet being significantly off course or suddenly encountering bad weather conditions. The cockpit crews of a modern jet can communicate by radio with traffic-control centers below, private phones on the ground, other planes in the air, and the passengers in the plane by simply flipping a switch on their instrument panels. The Visual Omni Receiver (VOR), a key navigational instrument located in the cockpit, is tuned to one of nine hundred–odd ground stations scattered across the United States. These provide a network of aerial guidelines. Pilots tune in to a station and then fly "on the beam" for the duration of the flight. The Air Traffic Control Transponder is a special radar unit built into every commercial aircraft.

It sends a clearly recognizable signal to air traffic control centers along the flight path, providing flight controllers with the airplane's exact location. Another navigational aid is the Automatic Direction Finder Receiver (ADF RCVR), which is used primarily for landings.[16]

The cost of the electronic equipment used for safer navigation on today's jets may run as high as $200,000. In 1939 commercial transport planes carried $12,000 worth of this equipment. The cost of airborne radar is about $25,000 per installation. The combined cost of installing a new navigation device known as Distance Measuring Equipment (DME) and radar identification transponders on the nation's civil air fleet is $40 million—approximately the cost of six jet liners. "The airlines are currently testing an airborne electronic device which constantly monitors important aircraft components and predicts when a malfunction will occur." [17]

From the moment a commercial airliner begins its take-off it is locked into the elaborate tracking systems maintained by the Federal Aviation Administration. Air traffic controllers at the airports and at various air-route centers constantly monitor their radar screens to make sure that each airplane is adhering closely to its flight plan. When the airplane approaches its destination, skilled flight controllers help the captain to land.

The Instrument Landing System (ILS) uses a combination of three radio systems to guide the airliner to a perfect landing. The pilot uses the "glide slope beam" to determine the correct angle of descent. The "localizer" beam, which intersects the glide slope beam vertically, leads the plane straight to the runway. Two vertical radio marker beams (set at distances of five miles and half a mile out) give the pilot his distance from the runway. The airport flight controller monitors the aircraft's approach on a radar

[16] H. Guyford Stever, James J. Haggerty, and the Editors of *Life, Flight* (New York: Time, Inc., 1969), pp. 118–119.
[17] Tipton, p. 13.

screen offering a three-dimensional view. He instantly alerts the captain if his plane is off the beam. Occasionally heavy traffic near a major airport will necessitate the use of a "holding pattern." This is a "clearly defined loop marked by a radio beacon, where planes can circle until there is a free runway." Planes circle in rungs, going from top to bottom. They are protected by air space almost twenty times as great as the air space they normally have. The air traffic controller is the only person who can give a plane permission to enter such an "aerial stack." [18]

THE AIRLINE INDUSTRY IN THE UNITED STATES

The airline industry is one of the largest in the United States. Airlines spend billions of dollars purchasing and maintaining airplanes, hiring and training crew members, and constructing passenger terminals, administrative buildings and airplane hangars. Maintaining the highest safety standard is of utmost financial importance to the airline industry. One dramatic accident may hurt an airline's business for months and even years. More than in any industry, "safety pays."

Boeing, McDonnell-Douglas, and Lockheed build most of the airplanes now in use by U.S. commercial airlines. The Boeing 707 and the McDonnell-Douglas DC-8 are the most frequently used four-engine jets on overseas and cross-country flights. They seat 147 to 155 passengers and cost approximately $8 million. (A "stretched" model of the DC-8, thirty-seven feet longer than the normal model, carries 250 passengers.) The Boeing 720, a slightly smaller version of the 707, is designed for medium ranges. The Boeing 727, a tri-engine jet, is used for shorter domestic flights. Its shorter take-off and landing help speed pas-

[18] For a vivid description of ILS, holding patterns, and aerial stacks, see Stever and Haggerty, pp. 130–144.

senger services. It costs about $5.5 million. The Boeing 737 and the DC-9, both twin-engine jets, fly route segments of 750 miles or less. The new Boeing 747 jumbo jets, which can accommodate 362 to 392 passengers, cost a minimum of $24 million. A 747 is 232 feet long and 20 feet wide. It weighs 112,880 pounds. Its huge interior holds passengers on two levels. The 747 has proved highly successful and will undoubtedly rival and possibly even surpass the 707 and DC-8 in popularity on long-distance flights.

AIRLINE MAINTENANCE OPERATIONS

Because the airlines have such a direct stake in ensuring flawless performance, they operate large maintenance centers to keep their planes in top working order. The U.S. scheduled airlines spent $141,354,000 on maintenance in 1950. In 1968, maintenance expenditures had risen to $1,195,000,000, or an average of about $520,000 per aircraft. The airlines employ an average of twenty-three aviation mechanics for each airliner in their fleets. Some airlines maintain on cards or tapes an electronic file on every functioning part that goes into their aircraft. The cards or tapes are run through a computer, which tells exactly when each part must be checked or replaced before the next overhaul. There are eighteen thousand key structural parts and more than five hundred thousand individual components in a modern jet liner.[19]

During the inaugural period of a new type of aircraft, maintenance men check vital parts of the airplane at every opportunity.[20] When the new jet amasses six thousand flying hours, it is given a complete examination by the airline's maintenance personnel. Not one system is over-

[19] Tipton, p. 12.
[20] For further descriptions of safety-testing procedures by aircraft manufacturers, see Stever and Haggerty, pp. 101–108.

looked during this exhaustive check. An initial visual inspection is supplemented by the use of X-ray equipment. In one test, high-frequency sound waves are directed through plane sections to check for any deviations from a previously established "correct" pattern. There is also a dye check to test for any subsurface cracks in the airplane's structural metal.

In order to ensure that their airplanes will continue to give highest performances, airlines follow rigidly prescribed maintenance schedules which typically include en route checks at every stop, preflight checks every sixty-five hours of flight time, cleaning of plane exteriors every five days, maintenance checks every eight hundred flight hours, engine overhauls every five thousand flight hours, and airframe overhauls every eight thousand flight hours.[21]

THE ROLE OF THE AIRLINE PILOT

Like the astronaut, the jet pilot is a highly skilled, well-trained technician. He must have a vast reservoir of experience upon which to draw in case of emergency, but under normal conditions he flies his airplane largely by means of sophisticated machines and instruments.

A popular misconception is that the pilot "drives" an airplane in much the same manner as most people drive their automobiles. In reality, an airplane pilot makes *no* decision solely on the basis of intuition, whim or impulse. He depends on his onboard instruments and the information he constantly receives by direct ground-to-air communications from FAA flight control centers. The pilot's decisions are never totally independent. Before taking any action he checks and double checks with the co-pilot, the flight engineer and ground control.

The airlines maintain stringent, selective policies in hir-

[21] Tipton, p. 12.

ing jet pilots. Most airlines require an average of seven years of flying experience, including more than 2,000 hours of actual flying in multiengine jets, before they consider hiring a pilot. Most pilots have attended college; many have one or more graduate degrees. Typically, their basic flying instruction is obtained in a branch of the military services. Training is a large factor in the improved airline safety record. "The U.S. scheduled airlines spend about 100 million a year for crew training." [22] Once a pilot is hired, he undertakes an intensive training program usually given at the airline's flight training center. These programs, which last for about three months, consist of classroom instruction, extensive training in airplane simulators, and actual flying experience.

In one interesting classroom training technique, pilots study the functioning of the various airplane "systems" (electrical, fuel, navigational, oxygen, etc.) by monitoring large glass panels containing full-color diagrams of each system. These graphically show how the system functions under any given circumstance.

Modern flight training centers rely heavily on the use of specially constructed airplane simulators to facilitate learning. "The new 747 simulators cost an average of $2.5 million. This is comparable to the cost of a DC-7 or a Lockheed Super Constellation [the largest piston aircraft]." [23] These simulators consist of exact replicas of jet cockpits. All instrument panels and gauges appear in exactly the same dimensions as on an actual airplane. The standard three-man crew (captain, first officer, and flight engineer) sit in their regular positions and monitor the various controls.

Color TV pictures of airports, runways and the surrounding countryside are projected onto a screen placed outside the cockpit windows. These visual images duplicate the pilot's views during real take-offs and landings.

[22] *Ibid.,* p. 15.
[23] *Ibid.*

Time, as well as weather conditions, is varied to enable the pilot to train for every possible flight condition—day or night, good weather or bad.

Mechanical aspects of flight are also duplicated by the simulators. All combinations of pitch, roll and yaw (horizontal and vertical movements of the aircraft) are reproduced. Radio communications systems function exactly as they do aboard an airplane. Simulator instructors imitate the speech of flight controllers from various parts of the world (American ATC "English" is about one third faster than the "English" of British flight controllers). During a typical week a pilot may "take off" and "land" thousands of times without actually leaving the ground. Simulators have proven themselves as economical, practical devices for training pilots. They reproduce flight dangers such as faults, failures or emergencies without risk to life or property.

The final part of the pilot's training course is his inflight training. ("The estimated cost of an hour's training in a 747 is more than two thousand dollars. This is approximately one fourth the cost of a college education and is two to three times that of the 707." [24]) Both pilots and flight engineers must demonstrate their ability to fly the aircraft under the most difficult test conditions. For example, they are required to fly jets above and below their normal operating speed limits, take off with only three engines and land on two engines. During these training flights, experienced senior officers evaluate their proficiency, skills, attitudes and responses to emergencies.

Each time a pilot is transferred to a different type of airplane he is required to go back to school to learn the special characteristics of the new aircraft. Pilots must have expert knowledge of all systems in the complex machines they operate.

Captains of commercial aircraft routinely undergo tests

[24] *Ibid.*

of their skills, both by the airlines and by FAA officials. Each year throughout his flying career a commercial airline pilot must requalify by passing two FAA physicals (at six-month intervals) plus one company physical. He must prove his flying skills during two instrument checks (at six-month intervals) and one flying check. Failure in any one of these six tests means forced retirement. As part of his preparation for these tests a pilot goes through a proficiency retraining program every six months.[25]

Airline pilots continue to improve their skills every year. Like doctors and lawyers they keep abreast of new developments, procedures, and techniques. This advanced training is not optional. It is mandatory and it continues until retirement!

The airlines pay high salaries to their pilots, commensurate with the professional standards they demand. Usually after a young pilot is hired and trained, he serves initially as a flight engineer or a first officer (co-pilot). The number of years needed to become a jet captain often exceeds the length of time required to become a practicing lawyer or physician. Few captains are under thirty. Many captains continue to pursue academic interests after graduating from college. Many have the equivalent of M.A. or even Ph.D. degrees in fields such as engineering. All are in excellent physical health.

A pilot is typically promoted to the rank of captain during his thirties. He begins by flying a 727 (or its equivalent), at an average salary of $30,000 per year. By the time he is in his late thirties a captain may be transferred to a 707 at an average of $35,000. Captains of 747s are usually at least forty-five years of age. These professionals, responsible for handling an airplane whose initial cost is $23,000,000, receive $55,000 or more yearly.

Since the 1960s there has been a considerable increase in night flying. At these times, pilots fly almost exclusively

[25] *Ibid.*, p. 16.

by means of computerized instruments. They must, however, be continually prepared to take over manual control should the need arise. Pilots who fly or have flown in a branch of the military often develop a spirit of discipline and comradeship. Cockpit crews of commercial airlines often retain this spirit. Having spent long hours training together, they develop a close, empathic communication (verbal and nonverbal) based on mutual respect.

STEWARDESS TRAINING

Since the quality of passenger service directly influences the number of customers who will patronize an airline—one bad experience with a stewardess may deter a passenger from ever flying on a particular airline again—all airlines try to provide maximum passenger service.

Airline stewardesses are carefully selected. Typically, they begin their training at nineteen. Their training program takes approximately six weeks. Classes are held in cabins which duplicate the interiors of all aircraft used by the airline. Here trainees serve complete meals in practice sessions that are videotaped for subsequent step-by-step review. The cabin simulator is equipped with working galleys. Stewardesses receive precise instructions on how to handle every conceivable passenger request. They are taught to allay passenger anxieties, no matter how trivial or ridiculous they may seem. Instructors stress the importance of conveying genuine interest in passengers rather than artificial congeniality. They teach the stewardess trainees how to maintain order and calm during emergencies. Some airlines have assigned male cabin attendants rather than stewardesses for flights over the polar routes. As part of their training they have to know how to shoot a seal and prepare it as a meal, as well as how to build an igloo! [26]

[26] *Ibid.*

Stewardesses undergo special training in emergency evacuation training. They are drilled in techniques for efficiently removing passengers from the cabin through emergency exits and escape chutes. In one training procedure cabin mockups are placed around a swimming pool to simulate conditions that would occur if a plane were forced to make an emergency ditching upon a body of water.

AIRLINE PLANNING FOR THE FUTURE

Airline management and senior staff devote much time and effort to anticipating future activities. Route planning is particularly important because it attempts to answer such key questions as where to fly, how often, with what type of aircraft, at what time of day, in the immediate future and in subsequent years.

Route planning is primarily concerned with anticipating the best markets for potential passengers. It is based on extensive market research and considers such factors as population trends, trade, living standards, and special events (such as international exhibitions). Today, tourists represent the greatest single source of potential air passengers. Route planning weighs the appropriateness of a given aircraft to a particular market. Will the present-day jet, the larger 747, the projected air buses, or supersonic jets attract more potential passengers? Airlines compare advantages and limitations of the different aircraft and purchase the type they believe will most efficiently serve their needs.

Two major U.S. aircraft manufacturers (McDonnell-Douglas and Lockheed) are nearing completion of a new type of aircraft which will probably begin service by late 1972—a multimillion-dollar "air bus" jet liner. McDonnell-Douglas' version is the DC-10; Lockheed's, the L-1011 TriStar. These trijet air buses are designed to carry 270 to 345 passengers (depending on seating arrangements). They will cost $14 to $15 million each.[27] The new planes will compete with the 747 jumbo jets on many high-volume, medium-range routes. Their cruising speed of 600 miles per hour is about the same as the 747's. The trijets are approximately 175 feet long and 19 feet wide; the 747 measures 231 feet in length and is 20 feet wide. The air buses will operate most profitably on routes of 250 to 1,500 miles. They will also be able to land in smaller airports that cannot accommodate the Boeing 747.[28]

McDonnell-Douglas designed the DC-10 with extra landing gear and tail clearance so that it can be "stretched" into an aircraft with intercontinental range. Lockheed's L-1011-8, an entirely new version of its standard air bus (the L-1011), will hold up to 400 passengers and will also be capable of intercontinental flights. A twin-engine air bus is being developed in Europe for airlines that require only a short-range jet.[29] Major airlines recently purchased new wheeled passenger lounges that will be used for the 747's and the new air buses at New York and other airports by 1971. These lounges are actually part bus and part elevator. They can pick up as many as 150 passengers from ground-level boarding areas or from the elevated boarding ramps now in use at most airports.[30]

THE ROLE OF THE GOVERNMENT IN MODERN COMMERCIAL AVIATION

Modern aviation is a joint venture of the Federal Aviation Administration, the Civil Aeronautics Board, the U.S. Weather Bureau, and the airlines.[31] Governmental agen-

[27] Robert A. Wright, *The New York Times,* July 18, 1970, pp. 29 and 31.
[28] *Time,* August 3, 1970, p. 64.
[29] Wright, p. 31.
[30] Robert Lindsey, *The New York Times,* June 2, 1970.
[31] Unless otherwise noted, all source material for this section comes from Bernardo, pp. 94–113.

cies take a leading role in coordinating and running the airline industry, insisting on rigorous adherence to their strict safety standards. The federal government, private research firms and the airlines currently have more than 500 individual projects under way directly related to air safety.[32]

The Civil Aeronautics Board (CAB) is an independent agency of the federal government, established in 1940 to regulate various economic and safety activities of U.S. domestic and international airlines. Its five members are appointed by the President, with the approval of the Senate. The CAB regulates air fares, frequency of services and mail-rate payments. It issues certificates (licenses) to U.S. domestic and international airlines. It also grants permits to foreign airlines servicing the United States. It sets aviation safety rules and aircraft safety standards. It cooperates with the Department of State in establishing international standards for safety and operations. The CAB is the agency responsible for maintaining reasonable and adequate public service in civil aviation.

The National Transportation Safety Board, a branch of the Department of Transportation, publishes statistical data and other information pertaining to commercial and private aviation. A special Bureau of Aviation Safety works to achieve improved air safety by investigating airplane accidents and determining their probable causes.

The Federal Aviation Administration (FAA) is the governmental agency within the Department of Transportation which deals directly with the daily functioning of airplane service. The FAA controls the ever-increasing amount of air traffic. It attempts to divide equitably all available air space between civil and military users. It is responsible for expanding, modernizing and improving the present federal airways system.

The long-range goal of the FAA is to ensure that all flyers enjoy the highest safety standards. As part of this

[32] Tipton, p. 14.

program, it modernizes airports. It oversees installation and use of advanced radar and other electronic equipment. It strives constantly to improve the accuracy of weather forecasting. It designs communications systems which will make possible more efficient automatic control procedures, further reducing the chance of human error. It recruits and trains air traffic controllers.

The Flight Standards Service of the FAA is chiefly concerned with the safety of airplane and airmen. It establishes safety standards which must be obeyed by manufacturers who design and build airplanes. It also maintains rigorous maintenance standards for all civil aircraft. Before any airplane designed for public use becomes operational it must pass flight tests given by this office. The Flight Standards Service also tests the qualifications of pilots, radio operators, flight engineers, mechanics, navigators, and dispatchers. It establishes training-school requirements for airplane mechanics. It checks all equipment used in flight (such as air navigational instruments, landing aids, radar, and communication facilities). FAA safety inspectors routinely observe commercial airline flights, sitting in a special "jump" seat next to the pilot. By viewing the crew in action the inspector can directly test the skills of each crew member.

The Systems Research and Development Service of the FAA works mainly to modernize the air traffic control system. A special experimental center in Atlantic City, New Jersey (the National Aviation Facilities Experimental Center), provides a realistic testing ground for many of the new innovations in air traffic control. The goal of this research is to link up all federal airways electronically so that sophisticated machines will be able to perform most of the operations of air traffic control under all weather conditions. Currently, air traffic controllers perform these tasks, but the rapid increase of airplane flights dictates the need for electronic equipment to ease their burden.

The use of new radar equipment will give pilots all

necessary information about take-off, inflight operations (including avoidance of bad weather conditions) and landing. It will also monitor the skies surrounding the airplane, indicating to the pilot the position of all traffic near his plane. This newly designed radar will be able to tell the pilot where he may fly safely to avoid any collisions. FAA officials are currently working to obtain the necessary funds for this and other types of modernization from the U.S. Congress. Future air traffic control will be made easier by the use of automatic air-to-ground communications, automatic printers, and special computers which will be capable of developing flight paths that will not conflict with those of other aircraft. Estimates for the full implementation of the program range from 1975 to 1980. When this electronic equipment is fully operational, the job of the air traffic ground controller will be greatly simplified. He will have to monitor only his equipment and make sure that the pilot is correctly responding to existing flight conditions. He will be able to devote all his energies to preventing accidents.[33]

The Installation and Material Service and the Systems Maintenance Service are the two FAA units specifically charged with the care of all equipment used in the nation's air traffic control and navigation systems.

The Air Traffic Service is probably the best-known unit of the FAA. Its jobs are to 1) control all air traffic, 2) establish and enforce appropriate rules and regulations, and 3) clearly designate and assign specific air spaces to users of the federal airways system. In addition to operating airport control towers the ATS also mans numerous air-route control and communication centers throughout the nation. This elaborate system ensures that planes will be carefully monitored throughout *every* phase of flight.

The Airports Service of the FAA works to keep airports in optimal operating condition and to maintain a national airport system capable of keeping up with all new develop-

[33] Paul J. C. Friedlander, "Electronics in the Wild Blue Yonder," *The New York Times,* May 17, 1970, travel section, p. 41.

ments in navigation, communication and air traffic control. Each year this service submits to the Congress a list of all airports necessary to maintain the national airport system. Then, pending Congressional approval, funds from the Federal Aid to Airports Program are made available for such items as acquisition of land, construction of runways and taxiways, renovation of administration buildings, revamping of customer terminals and obtaining a more efficient flow of automotive and bus traffic to and from airport buildings. Usually the federal government pays half of the cost; matching funds are provided by the airport sponsors.

The Aircraft Development Services of the FAA is concerned with the safety and reliability of airplanes built by aircraft manufacturers. As we mentioned before, most U.S. commercial airplanes are built by three companies: Boeing, McDonnell-Douglas, and Lockheed. It often takes years of research before these manufacturers can submit design specifications and blueprints for a new aircraft to this office of the FAA. Once the original plan for a new aircraft is endorsed by the FAA, its engineers work along with factory engineers at every phase of construction. The various parts of the airplane (fuselage, wings, nose, tail surfaces and landing equipment) are continually checked for quality and adherence to the approved original plan. FAA and factory engineers work together to scrutinize the construction of the aircraft's engines, its many flight controls and instruments, and its interior design. No part of the airplane is built without routine checks and double checks.

During these routine checks parts of the airplane are often modified to keep up with improved design specifications. Pilots have a lot to say about new aircraft design. One of the most popular of today's airliners incorporated 57 of the 63 changes in cockpit layout recommended by a pilot-evaluation committee.[34]

Once a new aircraft is constructed, it undergoes a thor-

[34] Tipton, p. 14.

ough ground testing. It is taxied on the runway and its various movable wing and tail parts are tested. Engine performance, operation of escape exits, and *every* other aspect of the airplane are carefully checked. At this point, any serious errors will be noticed. Poorly operating systems may be modified or replaced completely. The aircraft must also pass rigorous tests of structural strength and safety at this point.

Special tests are designed for the wings of new airplanes. Sections of wings are cut with metal saws and then subjected to regular applications of pressure, simulating the stresses that occur in flight. In other laboratory tests they are bent repeatedly to test the limit of pressure they can endure before buckling.[35] "The wings on a jetliner can carry a load of automobiles stacked as high as the Washington Monument." [36]

In order to ensure that the metal along the fuselage will not develop even tiny cracks while subjected to constant changes in pressurization, a special technique called "hydrofatigue" testing has been developed. As the name implies, this is a test to measure the amount of repeated stress the fuselage will tolerate before it begins to show signs of wear (cracks). The fuselage of the aircraft tested is lowered into a form-fitting tank of water. The cabin inside the fuselage is sealed as in normal flight. Water is then pumped in until the pressure the plane would maintain in flight is reached. This takes about one minute. One minute later, the water is pumped out. Thus the cycle of pressurization change undergone in a normal flight is duplicated in a span of two minutes.[37] The hydrostatic tests on a jet liner put the structure through the equivalent of one hundred years of flight operations! [38] After these tests have been successfully completed, the airplane receives an "Ex-

---

[35] Stever and Haggerty, p. 107.
[36] Tipton, p. 14.
[37] Stever and Haggerty, p. 106.
[38] Tipton, p. 12.

perimental Certificate of Airworthiness" from the FAA.

The Federal Aviation Administration also has an Office of International Aviation Affairs which coordinates FAA's activities overseas. Its activities include sending air safety specialists to foreign countries and establishing free training programs in the United States for foreign aviation personnel. This unit of the FAA is the representative of the International Civil Aviation Organization (ICAO), a specialized agency of the United Nations, based in Montreal. The ICAO was established in 1947 to bring about increased cooperation in international air transportation. It serves to promote uniform operating and safety procedures among nations. Its member nations operate more than 90 percent of all international airlines.

WHAT IS BEING DONE TO PREVENT HIJACKING

In response to a rash of aircraft hijacking during the first half of 1970, governmental authorities, airline associations, and individual carriers joined together to develop methods for deterring hijackers. They are understandably reluctant to discuss these protective measures publicly so as not to aid potential hijackers.[39]

Pre-flight screening methods have proven themselves highly effective. Typically, these involve stationing observers in airport ticket areas, walkways, and waiting areas. These observers are trained to spot personality traits—"behavioral tipoffs"—known to characterize hijackers. If a passenger exhibits one of these "tipoffs," airport officials ask him to walk through an area where a magnetometer is installed. This electronic sensor detects metal objects, such as guns and knives, on passengers or

[39] John Brannon Albright, "Skyjackings: What's Being Done and How Passengers React," *The New York Times,* June 21, 1970, travel section, p. 3.

in baggage. If the passenger has a significant amount of metal on his person, a blue light flashes. He is then subjected to interrogation, search and possible arrest by U.S. marshals or other law-enforcement officials. A coordinated pre-flight screening system, designed to protect all commercial flights within an airport, went into operation at New Orleans International Airport in July, 1970.[40]

Other measures to prevent hijacking include X-raying of checked baggage before it is loaded into the hold of a plane and a thorough examination of all hand baggage. Occasionally, armed plainclothes guards, disguised as passengers, fly on regularly scheduled flights. Airlines which have had previous incidents of sabotage follow especially tight security measures. Liaison is established with governmental authorities in all countries where the airline operates. At some airports police surround the airline's aircraft and passengers are bused from the terminal directly to the plane.

There is growing pressure for the adoption of a worldwide agreement on the prosecution and punishment of anyone interfering with the operation of an airplane. The International Civil Aviation Organization, which has a membership of 119 nations, held a conference in Montreal on this problem in the summer of 1970. It made plans for another convention which will specifically deal with the prosecution of hijackers. The Legal Committee of the United Nations General Assembly has adopted a resolution urging all governments to guarantee that air pirates will be prosecuted.[41]

AIR SAFETY

The following excerpts from a speech by Stuart G. Tipton, president of the Air Transport Association of Amer-

[40] UPI, "Airport Sets Up Hijacker Screen," *The New York Times,* July 17, 1970.
[41] *The New York Times,* June 21, 1970.

ica, help to integrate much of the information on air safety contained in this chapter: [42]

How Safe Is Flying?

What I'm going to appeal to is your sense of logic, your inherent fairness, your ability to judge facts. And right off the bat, I'm going to admit one thing: Flying, like everything else we do, has an element of danger.

Now, having conceded that flying can be hazardous —by all the rules of inevitable logic—I think we also can assume that flying is not the only sinner. There is an element of risk in virtually everything we do. People get killed taking baths, driving automobiles, taking walks, riding bicycles, smoking cigarettes.

In a sense, nothing in this world of ours is completely, totally, 100 percent safe. Not even sitting in a house, just eating and sleeping, and never going out. Safety in itself is merely the art of reducing risk to the least possible chance of occurrence. . . .

Fear as a Factor in Air Travel

We in the industry are only too well aware of the fact that some Americans are afraid to fly. The U.S.-scheduled airlines carried more than 162 million passengers last year. But many of these were repeaters. In other words, the airlines sold more than 162 million individual tickets, but they carried a much smaller number of individuals. This leaves a considerable segment of the population that could afford to fly, but doesn't. Fear, certainly, is one of the major factors.

I suspect there are some of you in the audience who are afraid to fly. Well, let's talk about fear. There was a time when the airlines didn't like to talk about it.

We don't mind talking about safety now. We're not afraid to talk about fear, because while we understand it, and even sympathize with it, we think it is unjustified —as far as flying is concerned.

Just why are people afraid to fly? Why are so many

[42] Tipton, pp. 1–11.

wives, for example, opposed to their husbands flying?

First, there's the belief that nobody walks away from an air crash. That phrase "There were no survivors"— I suspect most of you believe it applies to the majority of air accidents. Obviously, it applies to *some* accidents. When a plane hits a mountain at three hundred miles an hour, there is no chance for survival . . . no more chance, I might add, than you'd have in a head-on collision in an automobile at sixty miles an hour. But the University of Miami just a few years ago studied more than two hundred crashes over a ten-year period. There were approximately 5,300 passengers and crew members involved in those two hundred accidents. More than 60 percent survived.

The truth is that most accidents *are* survivable. They occur under conditions that permit survival. And the airlines, as well as the federal government, are doing everything possible to increase the chances of walking away from a crash because they recognize that planes can and do get into trouble.

Greater Crash Survival a Goal

For example, no flight attendant is released from an airline's emergency training program until she has demonstrated complete knowledge of the airplane's emergency facilities and procedures. After this training and her initial flight assignments, she is given refresher training and periodic competence checks. In fact, prior to the departure of many flights of U.S. overseas carriers, cabin attendants are quizzed to be certain that they have retained their training on how to handle emergencies. In any case, where a flight attendant indicates a lack of the necessary knowledge, she is immediately sent back to training before further flight assignment.

The domestic airlines, as well as our international flag carriers, require stewardesses to take recurrent training in emergency procedures at least once a year. They are brought up to date on revised or new procedures, and they also take refresher courses in what they learned in stewardess school. There are no exceptions. A stewardess who has been flying for ten years still must take recurrent training.

Right now, government and industry are engaged in a massive research program aimed at one goal: to increase your chances of surviving an emergency that results in an accident. To lessen the chances of fire after impact. Improved evacuation chutes. Better marking of emergency exits. Stronger seats. With the exception of preventing mid-air collisions, there is no area of safety getting more attention than crash survival. In brief, you have a very good chance of walking away— and it will not be long before the words "very good" will be changed to "excellent."

I mentioned the rigid, even ruthless training of cabin attendants. Let's take a brief look at the men up front. I wonder how many of you regard yourselves or your husbands as expert drivers . . . or even as good drivers. I'm going to make a statement that may surprise you. There is not a single person in this room, no matter how well he or she can handle an automobile, who is one tenth as capable of flying.

Pilot's Training as Long as Doctor's

Did you know that it takes as long or longer for a pilot to qualify for command of an aircraft as it does for a doctor to qualify for practice? Seven years is the average time a co-pilot serves before he wears the coveted four stripes of a captain. And his training never stops. His flying ability and his capability for command are tested twice a year by special check flights and by comprehensive examination. He may have flown for 25,000 hours, but he still has to go through recurrent training every twelve months, and that training includes the testing of his ability to handle emergencies.

He cannot fly a specific route unless he has qualified over that route—to make sure he is familiar with the airport's navigation aids, approach patterns and other route characteristics.

Sometimes it strikes us that those who are afraid to

fly are guilty of being illogical. Most of us think nothing of stepping into our own car, supremely confident of our ability to drive. Yet the average motorist can encounter more emergency situations in one day of driving than an airline pilot might encounter in months of flying. And this average motorist cannot even approach the airline pilot in his ability to cope with any emergency—not in his physical reactions, in his technical skills nor in his split-second judgment.

As I said earlier, safety is the art of reducing risk to the least possible chance of occurrence. Flight crew training is a major reason why commercial aviation *is* safer.

Let's discuss another fear. Fear of something going wrong with an airplane. Well, things *do* go wrong with airplanes. Nobody has ever invented a machine that is totally foolproof. But go back to the analogy of your automobile versus an airliner. I'll venture to say that of the drivers in this audience, there is not a single person who has not at some time stepped into a car that had a major mechanical fault involving potential danger. Worn tires, because the family budget may have been a bit strained. Brakes that needed relining, because you just hadn't gotten around to taking the car to the garage. Windshield wipers that needed replacing. A burned-out headlight. Tired shock absorbers.

Do you think that any airline would allow one of its planes to take off with corresponding mechanical faults? The airlines have what they call "no-go" items—and these simply are maintenance items directly affecting safety. If there is the slightest suspicion that any one of these components should be listed as "no go," that aircraft will not move one inch until it is fixed.

Preventive Maintenance for Safety, Reliability

We might term this precautionary. An airline creed of equal importance is prevention—to catch mechanical troubles before they become troubles. I'm sure those of you who have flown have been annoyed by a delay caused by mechanical malfunctions. I'm also sure that you never stopped to realize that the reason our airlines operate on schedule about 80 percent of the time is due to preventive maintenance. And I'm sure also that if you were privileged—and I use that word deliberately— if you were privileged to visit the maintenance base of any scheduled airline in the United States you would be flabbergasted at the extent of this prevention.

You would see planes literally taken apart and rebuilt. You would see key structural parts X-rayed. You would see many components replaced even *before* they showed signs of wear. There is no such thing as an old airliner. Since maintenance chores on an airliner are planned far in advance and done on schedule, the airliners are in tip-top condition all the time.

Suppose your car was a modern airliner, and you decided to maintain it as the airlines maintain their aircraft. You'd need three full-time mechanics. You'd inspect the car before every drive—even to the shopping center around the corner. You'd replace all four tires every five hundred miles. You'd tune the engine every twenty-five hundred miles. Every ten thousand miles you'd disassemble most of the engine, change the brake linings and take the transmission apart, looking for any sign of wear. At twenty-five thousand miles you'd install a completely new engine.

It costs an airline almost three quarters of a million dollars a year to keep a 707 or DC-8 in good operating condition. This is more than the total cost of a new transport plane less than twenty years ago.

Our scheduled carriers are spending $3.3 million a day on maintenance, and one third of their work force is concerned with the care and feeding of airliners. The overhaul time of just a single jet engine is fifteen days, requiring ten mechanics to disassemble the engine and fifteen to put it back together. For every hour of flight a commercial transport plane receives five man hours of maintenance.

Still worried about something going wrong with an airplane? I repeat: Safety is the art of reducing risk to the least possible chance of occurrence.

Are you afraid of mid-air collisions? We wouldn't blame you after reading or hearing all the talk about our crowded skies and the collision menace. But let's be logical about this, too. The airlines operate fifteen thousand flights a day. In any given year there are almost sixty million take-offs and landings at airports where the Federal Aviation Administration maintains control towers. And these airports represent only three percent of the nation's total civil airports! There are 2,300 airliners, 136,000 private and business aircraft and 32,310 military planes using our air space. At any given hour there may be at least 18,000 human beings traveling through this air space at speeds of up to 625 miles an hour.

Odds Against Air Collision 1 in 6,600,000

Now, weigh these rather astronomical figures against the number of fatal collisions involving scheduled airlines: less than a dozen. All this boils down to a simple statistical fact: Compare the number of flights flown, say, since 1938 with the number of fatal collisions involving airliners, and the odds against such a tragedy are about one in 6.6 million. How would you like those odds for your own automobile?

But the airlines are working on reducing even these odds. After years of research and testing, they will, in the next couple of years, place into service a CAS— Collision Avoidance System. CAS will, basically, warn a pilot when he is on a collision course with another plane and tell him what to do to avoid it.

No one, least of all the airline industry, denies that faults exist in our air traffic control system. But what too many people don't realize is that the faults largely result in inefficiency—in delays and inconvenience, not in danger. The system just won't accept any more traffic than it can handle safely.

Yes, there are near misses. They stem from inadequacies in the air traffic control system due to human carelessness or human error. But near misses should be kept in perspective. They literally are accidents that did *not* happen. And many times they did not happen simply because safeguards built into the system recognized whatever mistake was made and soon enough to correct the error.

Are you afraid of weather? There are ten times as many flights operating safely today as there were fifteen or twenty years ago—and they're operating under weather conditions that fifteen or twenty years ago might well have grounded them. We're landing planes routinely under ceiling and visibility restrictions that were considered impossible just a few years ago. Our navigation aids, runway lighting, weather reporting—they've all been improved to the point where the airlines last year completed 97 percent of the scheduled mileage. And as in air traffic control, major improvements are just over the blue horizon—we expect to achieve, within the next five years, the capability of operating safely under near zero-zero ceiling and visibility conditions. In other words, all-weather flying.

We are also working on changing the weather whenever we can. For example, fog is now routinely being dispersed at a number of airports to clear the way for airline operations.

There has been fear expressed about new types of airliners . . . the idea that they usually develop bugs —design flaws—which result in fatal accidents. Well, they have on some rare occasions—occasions, by the way, which taught the industry a lot about its aircraft design and development program!

I said earlier that you would be flabbergasted if you could see an airline maintenance base. You would be even more flabbergasted if you could witness the incredible testing of a new airliner . . . testing which includes its deliberate destruction to determine exactly how much punishment it can take.

I'll cite one example and you may find it hard to believe. The most an airliner's wings move up and down— even in the most violent, severe turbulence—is two feet. In testing a jet liner recently, engineers bent the wings nine feet out of their normal position—and the wings still held. The weight applied to the wings in this test was more than 425,000 pounds—the equivalent of dropping fifty Cadillac cars on top of each wing to see if it would hold.

Airliners Put Through Tortuous Flight Tests

The flight tests to which new transports are subjected would frighten a bird. They involve maneuvers which no sane pilot would dream of attempting. You hear about bugs that develop in spite of all the testing. You never hear about the countless bugs that are eliminated by the most thorough research and development program in the world. If your new car were put through the equivalent of an airliner testing program, it would cost about twenty-five thousand dollars. And when you were to pick up your new car, you yourself would spend two days testing it before accepting it for your use.

The new jumbo jet that just began service this past January [1970], the Boeing 747, was put through a flight-test program that involved five aircraft, cost twenty-eight million dollars and lasted a year. These five aircraft logged fourteen hundred flight-test hours in the air, and two other structurally complete airframes underwent additional tests on the ground.

Robert Serling, well-known aviation writer, sums up the care that has gone into the design of the 747 in his recent book on airline safety, *Loud and Clear*. He says, "Every component going into this twenty-million-dollar monster is being approved by something new in airframe manufacturing—a special committee of five hand-picked safety experts. . . . The smallest, most outwardly insignificant item goes under the careful analysis of the safety group."

I know I keep comparing automobiles to airplanes. I do it deliberately, because the automobile is familiar to you and the airplane is not. This, as a matter of fact, is one source of fear—flying is a totally different dimension, an unfamiliar dimension, and unfamiliarity breeds apprehension.

But this is exactly why fear of flying is just as unjustified as it is understandable. It is, in its purest sense, a form of transportation with basically the same safety problems as the automobile. To be safe, it requires human skill, careful maintenance, adherence to traffic rules, and well-built equipment. I hope you agree by now that in every category the airliner far exceeds the automobile—even though few, if any, of you, would hesitate to get into your own car or somebody else's car.

And just why should you be afraid to step into a scheduled airliner? Because there were 135 passenger fatalities in U.S.-scheduled carrier accidents last year? Because the black headlines that inevitably accompany a major air tragedy shocked you and jolted you?

No airline person would blame you. An air disaster shocks and jolts the industry too. Nobody can be complacent about 135 deaths.

Yet, while some of us decry air crashes, while a large segment of the public tells us "I'm afraid to fly," there is a very real tendency to forget that people also get killed outside airplanes.

Each year about 55,000 Americans are killed in automobile accidents; 20,000 die from falls of various descriptions—ranging from slipping in bathtubs to falling off ladders; 2,600 are killed accidentally by firearms; more than 1,500 die in automobiles hit by trains; 3,600 are killed in vehicle accidents on farms and another 2,100 die just working on farms; about 800 are killed on bicycles; 7,400 drown while swimming or boating.

In all, about 113,000 Americans die each year while performing such everyday, presumably safe activities as taking a bath, riding in an automobile, working around the house, or riding a bicycle.

113,000 Killed Accidentally—135 in Airliners

I venture to say that among those 113,000 unfortunate persons are a considerable proportion who insisted that taking an airplane flight was dangerous. It seldom dawns on us that our prosaic, peaceful and harmless tools of travel and work kill far more people than the commercial airplane.

You might argue that I'm not exactly objective about air safety. All right, let's take the word of the most objective person in the world. Objective isn't even the best way to put it. Cold-blooded is more like it. The insurance underwriter. He wouldn't bet on the house in a Las Vegas casino. How does he feel about scheduled air travel?

Insurance companies once charged a dollar for every five thousand dollars worth of flight insurance. They now offer twenty thousand dollars worth of flight insurance for fifty cents—which is four times the protection for one half the price. What they're actually quoting you are odds of at least forty thousand to one that you will complete your trip safely. The odds are conservative, because the fifty-cent premium includes such underwriting costs as commissions, profits, and airport rent.

Insurance companies don't bet on unknown quantities. They follow the laws of probability as rigidly as the earth follows the law of gravity. This is why an airline pilot today pays the same life-insurance rates as a grocery clerk or bank teller or any other citizen whose daily exposure to danger approximates that of a bridge player. The same is true for stewardesses.

Airliner Twenty-four Times Safer than Car

Yet these airline people fly about eighty hours a month under all kinds of weather, all kinds of operating conditions, in all types of equipment from DC-3s to the big jets. If one thinks that flying exposes you to danger, then pilots and stewardesses would seem to be bucking the odds. The insurance companies say no. I don't ask you to take my word for it. But I humbly suggest that you at least consider their verdict on the safety of air travel. Based on the 1969 safety record of the U.S.-scheduled airlines, which was the third safest year in the history of commercial aviation, you have a 99.99992 percent probability of completing any flight safely. And if you don't like those odds, let me assure you that if you step into your own automobile, the odds are about twenty-four times less favorable. . . .

Safety is the art of reducing risk to the lowest chance of occurrence. . . .

CHAPTER 4

What Is a Phobia?

I SHALL ATTEMPT IN THIS chapter to give you some understanding of the psychological mechanisms involved in phobias. If you understand how phobias develop and maintain themselves, you will be in a better position to comprehend the flying phobia that is discussed at length in Chapter 5. I hope that in reading this chapter you will not only obtain a better grasp of the flying phobia itself but also gain some understanding of any other phobic reactions you may have. Helping yourself deal with these other phobias will help you to cope with the flying phobia and vice versa.

DIFFERENCES BETWEEN FEARS AND PHOBIAS

What is the difference between a normal fear and a phobia? A normal fear is a reaction which occurs in situations that would be frightening to most people. Thus, for example, if a stranger suddenly pointed a gun at you and threatened to kill you, it would be perfectly normal to experience fear, since this situation would frighten anyone. As a matter of fact, not to be frightened under these circumstances would be rather odd.

In a phobic reaction, by contrast, you experience an extreme dread in the presence of stimuli which would not bother or perhaps even be noticed by most people. While undergoing a phobic reaction you are fully aware that your fear is unrealistic, you know that the degree of anxiety you feel is totally incommensurate with the objective situation, yet you are emotionally convinced that nothing you can do will relieve the anxiety, except to escape! In a phobic reaction you experience a wide variety of physical symptoms such as heart palpitations, respiratory difficulties (holding of the breath, rapid breathing, choking sensations), digestive disturbances (nausea, vomiting, diarrhea), shaking, trembling, shuddering, sudden feelings of weakness, increased irritability to sounds and lights, profuse sweating, cold hands, headaches, dizziness and insomnia.

In addition to its being manifestly inappropriate, a phobia is distinguished from a fear by the *intensity* of the anxiety felt. Your surface behavior may appear relatively organized to the casual observer, but internally you experience dread, panic and terror. Your anxiety mounts uncontrollably. You may feel that your whole personality is on the verge of disintegration. *You react as if your life were at stake!*

Phobic reactions are extremely common in young children. Indeed, it is a rare person who at some time or another in his childhood has not experienced some temporary phobic reactions. Some children develop phobias in the first few months of life. (It is possible that certain people are more predisposed to phobic reactions than others, but very little is understood about constitutional factors in phobias.) Some phobias continue unabated throughout a lifetime unless treated; others are transitory and may, for seemingly mysterious reasons, disappear by themselves. Many of the phobias which occur in young children are "learned phobias." These are phobias the child copies from his parents or develops himself as a result of some highly unpleasant incident, such as being thrown from a horse.

In general, childhood phobias are less serious than phobias which develop later in life.

It is difficult to draw a fine line between universal fears and common phobias. Most of us, for example, have experienced fears of the dark, being left alone, death, old age, or fatal illness. But since these fears are shared by so many people, we do not ordinarily consider them pathological, unless they become exceptionally intense and persistent. Practically any stimulus or any situation may trigger a phobia. Certain "excitants" are especially likely to trigger phobic reactions.

Following is a list of some of the more common phobic excitants. This list is compiled from phobias I have personally observed in my patients or have gleaned from the psychiatric literature.[1] Some of these phobias have quaint-sounding technical names. Since these may be of interest to some readers, I will include them, but I should tell you that the current trend is not to give technical names to phobias. The list of potentially phobic stimuli is so large that to give each one a separate name can become ludicrous.

[1] If you wish to read further about phobias, I would recommend the following sources: Otto Fenichel, *The Psychoanalytic Theory of Neurosis* (New York: Norton, 1945); Sigmund Freud, "Analysis of a Phobia in a Five-Year-Old Boy," *Collected Papers* (New York: Basic Books, 1959), III, 149–289; Paul Friedman, "The Phobias," *American Handbook of Psychiatry*, ed. Sylvano Arieti (New York: Basic Books, 1959), Vol. I; Lucio E. Gatto, "Understanding the Fear of Flying Syndrome: Psychic Aspects of the Problem," *United States Armed Forces Medical Journal*, V (1954), 1093–1116; Emil A. Gutheil, *The Handbook of Dream Analysis* (New York: Liveright, 1970); Evelyn P. Ivey, "Recent Advances in the Psychiatric Diagnosis and Treatment of Phobias," *American Journal of Psychotherapy*, XII (1963), 35–50; Joseph Wolpe, *The Practice of Behavior Therapy* (New York: Elmsford, 1969); and Manuel D. Zane, "How One Psychiatrist Utilizes His Tape Recorder with Patients," *Frontiers of Clinical Psychiatry*, December, 1969.

COMMON PHOBIAS

Frightening Stimulus or Situation Technical Name

Frightening Stimulus or Situation	Technical Name
DEATH	
FEAR	Phobophobia
TRAVEL (planes, cars, ships, other vehicles)	Vehicular phobia
CONFINED SPACES (elevators, subways, tunnels)	Claustrophobia
HEIGHTS (high buildings, mountains, bridges, stairways)	Acrophobia
CROWDS	
PHYSICAL HARM	
GOING CRAZY	
DARKNESS	Nichtophobia
LIGHTNING	Astrophobia
FIRE	Pyrophobia
THUNDERSTORMS	Brontophobia
FALLING ASLEEP (being anesthetized, taking drugs, sleeping pills, etc.)	
BEING LEFT ALONE	
STAGE FRIGHT (being watched)	
TOUCHING	
BLUSHING	Erythrophobia
ILLNESS	Pathophobia
HEART ATTACK	
HEARTBEAT (palpitations)	
FEVER	
BLOOD	
WOUNDS	
HOSPITALS	
FIGHTS	
TIME OF DAY	
MOODS OF WEATHER	
LANDSCAPES	
LIGHTS AND SHADOWS	

Frightening Stimulus or Situation   Technical Name

RHYTHMIC SOUNDS	
BEING RUN OVER	
CANCER	Cancerphobia
SYPHILIS	Syphilophobia
GERMS	Microphobia

SHARP POINTED INSTRU-
    MENTS (knives, scissors,
    etc.)
	Aichophobia

ANIMALS (snakes, insects, etc.)	Zoophobia
CATS	Ailurophobia
SCHOOL	
EXAMINATIONS	

Any one of the above phobias may be precipitated during a flight. In general, the phobias which appear earliest on the list are most likely to be triggered on a flight and to become associated with the flying phobia. However, in special instances, a phobia far down on the list may be activated. For example, a particular passenger could conceivably develop a fear of the knife served to him with his meal, or become frightened of catching germs from an adjacent passenger, or develop a fear that a cat or some other animal stored in the baggage compartment might come into the cabin.

Fear of death is, of course, sufficient in itself to induce panic. If the flyer is, additionally, phobophobic, he will panic even more the moment he experiences marked anxiety. Claustrophobia is especially frightening while aloft because the flyer is robbed of the *one* alternative he believes could reduce his anxiety: physical escape.

If two or more phobias are triggered simultaneously the flyer's anxiety escalates enormously. As soon as he escapes one excitant, he is immediately confronted by another!

I would like you to recall for a moment the fears listed

in Chapter 2. It probably has occurred to you by now that many of these apparently random fears are actually manifestations of common phobias.

Try to match the fears listed in Chapter 2 with the phobias just outlined. Pay particular attention to your own set of fears and see which phobia or phobias they most closely approximate. Rank your fears in terms of intensity. Which is the most frightening to you? Which comes next? Do you have just one phobic reaction or several?

PSYCHODYNAMICS OF PHOBIAS

Phobias have always afflicted human beings. Their manifest content varies, of course, with cultural factors. A person living in a jungle would not be afraid of elevators or of subways, but he might be terrified of lightning or thunderstorms.

Until the twentieth century nobody understood these strange phenomena. Sigmund Freud first clarified the psychological mechanisms involved in phobias more than sixty years ago in a classic article entitled "Analysis of a Phobia in a Five-Year-Old Boy." [2] This article describes the case of a boy named Hans who had developed a fear that a horse would bite him in the street. Freud deduced from his study of the case that Hans had developed death wishes toward his father just prior to the eruption of his phobia. (Death wishes are not at all uncommon in children and, as is well known, represent one aspect of the Oedipus complex.) Because he felt guilty at harboring these death wishes, Hans repressed them—that is, he pushed them out of awareness. Despite this repression, he remained fearful that he would be punished for having such thoughts. He then unconsciously substituted the

2 Freud, pp. 149–289.

horse for his father. By attaching his fears to a horse, which he could easily avoid, he avoided awareness of his hostility to his father. He also avoided fancied retaliation from his father as well as from his own conscience.

This case illustrates certain basic features of all phobic reactions: [3]

1. *A pre-existing conflict exists within the person.* Most often this conflict is between his impulses (usually sexual, aggressive or a combination of both) and his "irrational conscience." The term "irrational conscience" refers to that part of the self which automatically and unconsciously throttles fantasies or impulses it regards as immoral or antisocial. It is similar to the Freudian concept of "infantile superego." Other terms used to describe this force are "cruel inner critic," "suicidal self," [4] and "top dog." [5]

The irrational conscience develops during the earliest years. It derives from childhood misperceptions and exaggerations of parental prohibitions. In adulthood it is partially supplanted by the "mature conscience" which weighs right and wrong according to reality principles, but it never leaves the person completely. It continues to operate within his psyche throughout his lifetime. The irrational conscience may direct large quantities of aggression or self-hate against the self without the person even knowing it! This aggression may be directed against the total self (as in the case of severe depressions), against specific thoughts or acts (inhibitions or phobias) or against parts of the body (impotence, frigidity, hysterical paralyses). The irrational conscience does not differentiate between the unbridled expression of sexuality and aggression and normal self-assertion. It clamps down on self-assertive acts

[3] Both Fenichel and Friedman discuss the psychoanalytic theory of phobias in considerable depth.

[4] Terms coined by Louis Paul in "The Suicidal Self," *Psychotherapy,* VII (1970), 177–180.

[5] Term coined by Frederick A. Perls in *Gestalt Therapy Verbatim* (Lafayette, Calif.: Real People Press, 1969).

(for example, taking a flight) as if they were crimes. Patients who become partially aware of their irrational conscience during psychotherapy, or spontaneously by themselves, describe it as violent, primitive, unreasoning and implacable. Typical images used to describe it are "hanging judge," "inquisitor," "Nazi persecutor," "homicidal maniac" and the like.

2. *The conflict is held in equilibrium by means of repression.* Each time the impulse or its accompanying fantasy comes closer to awareness, it is repressed (rendered unconscious). The person remains unaware of the content of his fantasies. Also, pleasurable sensations associated with the impulse are converted into feelings of anxiety and pain. As long as the person remains unaware of his impulses and fantasies, he can indefinitely avoid punishment from his irrational conscience.

3. *A seemingly innocuous external situation mobilizes the conflict.* Certain features of the external environment *symbolically* represent a) temptations to act out the repressed impulses, b) threatened punishments for these feelings, or c) both. Since the person is already in a state of tension due to the anxiety engendered by the repressed conflict, he is especially susceptible to the sudden eruption of panic. The external stimulus is like a match lighting a powder keg.

4. *The person is fully aware of his anxiety in the phobic situation.*

5. *He is unaware, however, of the relationship between the phobic situation and the underlying struggle between impulses and irrational conscience.* By maintaining his repression he avoids coming to grips with what is really bothering him.

6. *He attaches his fears to some aspect of the external situation that is seemingly far removed from the original target of his impulses.* This process is called displacement. The external situation is, of course, symbolically connected with the originally feared object. An example

of this is Hans's becoming afraid of a horse instead of his father. It is another device to keep the basic conflict unconscious.

7. *Instead of perceiving the danger as emanating from within he focuses on external threats.* This process is called projection. The person projects his irrational conscience (he feels somebody or something wants to harm him). He also projects his own inner anxiety and excitement ("lightning will strike the plane"). The main function of projection is to reduce anxiety by removing the locus of danger from within the person to the outside world. It is easier to deal with identifiable external dangers than to cope with mysterious internal ones.

8. *He may regress to earlier modes of adjustment.* He may, for example, become inordinately dependent on some person or 'agency.[6] This process is called regression. Thus a person who is afraid to leave his house alone (agoraphobia) may be able to do so if accompanied by somebody on whom he has become dependent.

9. *As soon as he removes himself from the phobic situation, anxiety abates and the underlying conflict remains in a state of repression.*

Although they are highly disturbing, phobic reactions have distinct advantages. They protect the individual from experiencing anxiety continuously since they manifest themselves only under special circumstances which can usually be avoided. Also, they permit the person to maintain ongoing relationships with people who are significant to him. He can discharge unacceptable feelings onto persons or things that have no apparent connection with the original targets of his unacceptable impulses.

The phobic person, in short, avoids coming to terms with what is really bothering him by shifting the threat from within himself to the outside world (projection) and by attaching his fears to stimuli which most people regard

[6] How therapists can capitalize on this dependency in working with the phobic flyer will be discussed in chapters 7 and 8.

as harmless but which have a symbolic relationship to repressed core conflicts (symbolization and displacement).

This is similar to the type of self-deception we engage in when we dream. One of the primary purposes of dreaming is to enable us to try to solve troublesome problems while continuing to sleep. If we did not dream, we would be up all night worrying instead of sleeping. In our dreams, we create the illusion that we are viewing a series of seemingly fantastic and irrelevant events. Occasionally, when our anxiety erupts in the form of a nightmare we sense that the "irrelevant" material has touched upon something very crucial in ourselves, but most often in dreams, as in waking life, we avoid facing troublesome parts of ourselves by denying them, by displacing the locus of the threat from within ourselves to outside forces, and by attaching our fears to innocuous external objects.

In recent years the theory that irrational guilt over unacceptable impulses lie at the root of all phobic reactions has been supplemented by an increased emphasis on the role of "separation anxiety." Certain people develop inordinate anxiety whenever they leave familiar surroundings. Such individuals become panicky if they even think of separating from people, places, things, or ideas on which they have become dependent. They also become very anxious if they have to engage in unfamiliar activities or to do things differently. Frequently they arrange their lives in such a way as to avoid drastic changes in the status quo. However, if some unforeseen event dislodges them from their familiar moorings, they react emotionally like the two-year-old child who, having lost his mother in a crowd, is convinced that he will never find her and will die.

In some instances when a patient describes a particular phobia the cause of his fear is rather apparent to the therapist. For example, if a male reports a problem of sexual impotence, we assume more or less automatically that he has irrational fears of women. Similarly, in the case of frigidity, we assume the woman fears the male's sexuality.

Most often, however, in working with phobias we have to do a great deal of detective work to find out what unconscious fears are involved. Fortunately, our task is made easier by the fact that we have been studying phobias for more than sixty years. On the basis of this clinical experience we are usually able to form a tentative hypothesis as to what is troubling a person from his description of his phobic symptom. Usually these hunches turn out to be essentially correct. Occasionally, however, we may have to revise them drastically as we find out more about the patient.

In summary, the anxiety in most phobias is generated by: (1) fears of retribution from one's irrational conscience for having sexual or aggressive thoughts or (2) separation anxieties or (3) some combination of both.

EXAMPLES OF UNCONSCIOUS CONFLICTS IN PHOBIC REACTIONS

Recently an elderly male patient consulted me because he had become fearful of leaving his home and walking on the streets alone (agoraphobia). Some months before he came to visit me his sister, who had catered to him for many years, became seriously ill. Without his being aware of it, he developed hostile feelings toward her. Unconsciously, he perceived her illness as depriving him of love. He then developed an unconscious plan: "If I incapacitate myself (by not being able to leave my house), she will have to take care of me again." As soon as he became aware of his unconscious resentment as well as the wish concealed by his phobia, his symptoms rapidly disappeared.

Another case comes to mind: A female entertainer developed severe stage fright (a common phobic reaction) shortly after her marriage. A number of components entered into this phobia: (1) She was afraid that if she sang professionally, her husband would no longer take care of her (separation anxiety). (2) She was also afraid that her physical attractiveness would arouse male members of the audience and lead to sexual acts (guilt over sexuality). (3) She was also fearful that she would be attacked by members of her audience if they became aware of her contempt for them (guilt over hostility).

A male patient who was a pathological gambler developed a vehicular phobia. He was unable to travel by any vehicle; he could only walk. He felt tremendous urges to gamble but was guilty about this because he did not want (consciously) to deprive his wife of needed financial support. By rendering himself incapable of getting to gambling casinos he was able, temporarily, to contain his impulses.

A female patient developed a fear of walking on the streets of New York (she had recently arrived from a foreign country). After talking with her for a while it became apparent that she was specifically afraid of fainting on the street. Allied to this was another fear that the person who revived her would see that her undergarments were not clean. She was able to recall that as a child her mother had frequently warned her to wear fresh undergarments at all times, because if she ever did faint on the street, people would criticize her for not being clean. For this woman, then, walking on the street symbolized both a temptation to expose herself and a fear of being punished. It also activated hostile feelings toward her mother.

Another woman with an elevator phobia (a form of claustrophobia) stated: "I am afraid that the elevator will get stuck and nobody will pay attention. I could be half dead in the elevator and nobody would care!" She recalled being stuck in an elevator with her father at the age of five. Her mother who was outside of the elevator panicked and screamed, but her father seemed to her to be completely unconcerned. She also remembered that at about the same age she almost drowned, and again, "My father was very cool and didn't even realize that I was upset." This patient's sister was quite hysterical, often "making scenes" in public. Consciously, the patient despised her sister's behavior. She resolved to be "cool" like her father. However, deep down she felt that her sister's hysterical behavior was really more effective in getting her father's attention than her own "coolness." Her elevator phobia provided her with an excuse to act the way her sister did in the hope of getting her father's attention.

These cases illustrate, I think, that most phobias have multiple determinants and that they are frequently used to affect people with whom one is closely involved.

In the next chapter we will be dealing specifically with the flying phobia. The most obvious characteristic of the flying phobia is that it prevents the person from going places and doing things that he would consciously like to do. This limitation of mobility is true of all phobias. The phobic person avoids certain situations, certain stimuli, and certain people in order to escape anxiety.

Sometimes a single phobia will suffice to hold all of one's anxiety in check. If this works, the phobic person is fortunate. In other instances, a single phobia cannot contain the anxiety and it may generalize into a network of phobias. Thus, some people who initially are afraid to climb stairs may develop fears of crossing bridges, going through tunnels, taking trains, walking on the street, etc. Eventually, they become prisoners of their phobias.

CHAPTER 5

The Flying Phobia

SYMBOLIC MEANING OF FLYING

FLYING ALWAYS HAS HAD and always will have a deep symbolic significance to man. This symbolic meaning is largely uninfluenced by technological advances in aviation. As we saw in Chapter 3, there is very little mystery in commercial aviation. Yet we still react unconsciously to flying as if it were a magical event.

Let us consider, for a moment, some of the words that we use to describe various aspects of *flight:* sky riding, take-off, winging, soaring, cruising, gliding, drifting, hovering, high altitude, sky writing, stunt flying, rolling, porpoising, power diving, diving, zooming, spiraling, looping the loop, buzzing, car hopping, thrust, speed of sound, jet power, take wing, wing one's way, take a flight, take to the air, navigate the air, ride the skies, break the sound barrier, be at the controls, fly by the seat of the pants, ascend, pull up, pull out, nose dive, come in for a landing. Some of the words associated with *aviator* are: airman, pilot, wingman, bird, birdman, jet jockey, barnstormer, stunt flyer, bird woman, eagle, American eagle, ace, chutist, jump master, Daedalus, Icarus. Words associated with *airplane* include: air bus, air coach, airliner, air cruiser, flying bedstead, flying carpet, flying platform, flying boat.

I think you will agree that many of these words connote feelings of power, freedom, pleasure, sensuality and sexuality.

It might be interesting for you to jot down, at this point, your own personal associations to the words: *flying, aviator* and *airplane*. It would also be helpful to write out any dreams or daydreams that you have ever had in connection with flying. Put these dreams aside temporarily. Their meaning will become clearer later.

Let us now see how the concept of flight has been symbolized in religion and mythology. You are familiar, I am sure, with the biblical story of the building of the tower of Babel. This story recounts an attempt on the part of man to build a tower that would reach up to heaven. God became displeased and demolished the tower. In Greek mythology we have the famous story of Prometheus. Prometheus sped through the heavens, lit his torch to the sun and brought fire back to earth for man's use. Zeus, the chief of all the gods, punished Prometheus by chaining him forever to a rock. Phaeton, another figure in Greek mythology, requested permission from his father, Apollo, the sun god, to drive the chariot of the sun for one day. Phaeton was unable to control the divine steeds and they began to tear up the heavens. Earth complained to Zeus, who hurled a thunderbolt, causing Phaeton to fall from the chariot to his death. Daedalus fashioned a set of feathered wings for himself and his son, Icarus. He warned Icarus to fly a course midway between heaven and earth—not too high, to avoid scorching his wings, and not so low as to wet them in the sea. Icarus did not heed his father's warnings. Instead, he swooped through the skies like a thunderbolt. When he came too close to the sun, the wax which bound his feathers to his body melted and he fell into the sea to his death. These myths, as well as many others, all have the same theme: If man flies too high, he will be punished by God or by fate.

Not all legends involving human flight involve punishment. Peter Pan flew through the air without painful consequences. Also, the sultans of Arabian mythology flew on their magic carpets without punishment. The difference is, I think, that these flights do not contain the theme of excessive ambition implicit in the previously described myths. Flight has always been associated with escape from an unpleasant, confining setting. So, for example, we have the famous prison song:

> If I had the wings of an angel,
> Over these prison walls I would fly.

SEX, FREEDOM, AND PLEASURE IN FLYING DREAMS [1]

Dreams, in my opinion, afford us deep insight into our basic feelings toward flight. I would like to cite the following dream of a female patient of mine who is a fearful flyer. I think it is an excellent example of how flying may be perceived as a pleasurable, sexualized experience:

"I was on a glider with about four or five other women who were young and very beautiful. They wore bright colors and were very fashionable-looking. We were all hanging on the outside of the plane, not the inside. The pilot was flying over the water and we were going 'Whee!' Somewhere a voice said 'Be careful, you are going to get hurt!' I said, 'Who cares? It's so beautiful!' We were all kind of joyful and playing and I did not care. I was not frightened. We were like children playing on an amusement-park ride."

This is a wish-fulfillment dream. The dreamer is, in fact, terrified of flying. It expresses a wish that she could

[1] Please note that the discussion of the dreams presented in this chapter largely focuses on their relevance to fear of flying. These dreams can be interpreted at many other levels. Also, their meaning may be considerably modified by the dreamer's associations to their manifest content. Exceptions to this are the interpretations of Mary's and James's dreams (see below). These are based not only on the manifest content of the dreams but also on a knowledge of the dreamers' life histories as they emerged in the course of psychotherapy.

fly with freedom and pleasure not only on the glider portrayed in the dream but in her life generally. Note the similarity between the theme of the dream and the mythological stories mentioned earlier. In both instances a pleasurable, exhilarating experience is accompanied by a warning from some external authority (really a projection of the dreamer's own "irrational conscience") that flying too high and enjoying too much pleasure is dangerous and will lead to punishment.

Here is another dream, this one by a male patient, which illustrates beautifully how flying can be associated with freedom, excitement and sensuality:

"Sometimes I'm in my bed, but always in a room in a house. I am able to fly at will anywhere in the room, at any height, by simply shifting my weight in the direction in which I desire to go. Slowly I realize that this flying is an absolutely unique, very real experience—more exciting and free than anything I have ever experienced. Sometimes in my dreams I fly through the window and it is even better, if that is possible."

This dream is reminiscent of the Peter Pan story; the dreamer actually loves to fly. His anxiety develops on the ground. He feels guilty whenever he surpasses his father.

Here is another dream which I think conveys a feeling of the freedom and pleasure inherent in flying:

"I started off in a version of my old prep school. We were not studying English or Latin as usual. Instead, we were learning how to ride air currents. I decided I wanted to fly to San Francisco. I had a particular interest in going on a vacation to a gambling casino near San Francisco. I started off on my trip and woke up halfway through."

This dreamer is, in fact, a very "earth-bound" person. His mode of living is highly conventional. He usually keeps himself "boxed in." The dream expresses his wish to be free. However, guilt feelings intervene and he wakes up "halfway through"; he is unable to carry out his plans. As is usually the case, one's attitude toward flying reflects one's over-all orientation to life:

"I was looking at the underside of a big powerful-looking aluminum airplane which was going through some great maneuvers in the sky. When it came down, it made a great 'loop the loop'—a great big spectacular maneuver. It made a beautiful 'sideslip' to come down for a perfect landing in the water near the coastline."

This individual is extremely potent in all aspects of his life except sexually; he has a life-long history of sexual impotence. He is expressing, in this dream, his wish to overcome his sexual problem. He is not afraid to fly.

In the dreams presented so far, the dreamer is totally oblivious to the realities of commercial aviation. Some of these dreams do not even include an aircraft! By contrast, the following dream by a male patient takes place aboard a modern plane, but, as you will see, it has nothing to do with aviation. Rather it reflects very personal fantasies.

"I was seated in a large plane, probably a Boeing 747, next to a woman who was obviously afraid of flying. I was attracted to her. She turned to me for help. I comforted her. Later on, I said to her, "Isn't it a shame that people make such a big deal about talking to strangers? It's really so easy to enter into an immediate friendship with a stranger!"

The patient, at the time he recounted the above dream, was going through a phase of expansiveness in his personal life. (Notice how this is expressed by his identification with the large, wide plane.) He was also becoming increasingly attracted to women outside of his marriage. This dream expresses his desire to "expand" as well as his fear that this will lead him into dangerous (extra-marital) relationships.

By contrast, note the following dream of a male patient:

"I was in a World War One plane. It had no top on it. It looked like the plane Snoopy flies in the Charlie Brown comic strip."

The patient's associations to this dream are significant: "I had this feeling of freedom, yet I was a little uncomfortable and felt silly. Anybody else would imagine himself in at least a 707, maybe a 747. All I could imagine was that I was in a obsolete World War One plane. I always feel uncomfortable going places by myself and leading a free existence."

Another dream in the same vein:

"I got into a little plane. It was very little—like a kid's plane. It went only thirty feet off the ground. It didn't go any higher. It could have gone higher, but I didn't let it."

Again, this dream reveals a lack of self-confidence. The dreamer sees himself as a little child and is afraid to permit himself to get very high off the ground.

The following dream by a female patient reminds me of the Jules Verne story *Around the World in 80 Days*:

"I was traveling on an endless ocean around the world in a balloon. The ocean was peaceful with the reflection of the sun. I reached an exotic island full of Negro inhabitants. I was disgusted with their primitive faces. I enjoyed it when I left the island and continued floating over the wonderful ocean full of happiness. I woke with a pitiful consciousness that my voyage was interrupted by dull reality."

This dream reflects a wish to float pleasurably by oneself. It also suggests fears of male sexuality. Finally, it indicates a desire to escape from the confines of a dreary, commonplace existence.

PSYCHODYNAMICS OF THE FLYING PHOBIA

Normally, when we embark upon a journey, we do so with the anticipation that it will be, at least temporarily, more pleasurable than our familiar surroundings. Most people fly for pleasure: to visit foreign places, to see new people, to meet relatives and friends, or to consummate profitable business deals. Why can't the phobic flyer enjoy these pleasures? Why does his flying become so fraught with pain and fear?

1. One reason is that *the act of flying reactivates latent separation anxieties*. It is impossible to deny, flying seven miles above the earth, that one has taken a giant step away from home base. Taking off, leaving terra firma, awakens fears of striking out on one's own, functioning independently, cutting ties with home. Symbolically, it represents leaving Mother. All people have some residual needs to stay close to Mother, to merge with her for security. Everyone experiences momentary anxiety when he leaves familiar surroundings, but most people accommodate rather quickly. Some people are aware of separation anxiety in themselves. Others remain unaware of it because they so arrange their lives that, for all intents and purposes, they never really leave home—even in fantasy. These are the "psychocentric" individuals described in Chapter 1. Still others go to the opposite extreme: They actively court danger. They seek to master their separation anxiety by showing themselves and others that they are not afraid. To do so they may become circus acrobats, "daredevil" pilots, parachutists, stock-car racers, etc. The technical term for these individuals is "philobats." [2] These "counterphobic" individuals become most anxious when forced to stay put. Many of them find it extremely difficult to establish and maintain intense personal relationships because they are constantly afraid that they may be trading their freedom for security.

A note about mothers who fly: They frequently are subjected to double doses of separation anxiety. In addition to feeling anxious about having left Mother Earth, they may be additionally burdened by feelings of guilt for having left their children behind.

2. As we saw in Chapter 4, *guilt reactions are crucial ingredients of all phobias*. If an individual has a particularly strong "irrational conscience," he will clamp down

[2] For further discussion of the psychodynamics of philobats, see Michael Balint, "Friendly Expanses—Horrid Empty Spaces," *The International Journal of Psychoanalysis*, XXXVI (1955), 225–241.

unmercifully on himself if he even *thinks* about sexual or hostile fantasies, much less carries them out.

Flying is often perceived unconsciously as a sexual act. The shape, speed, power and vibrations of a plane, as well as its trajectory from ground to air, all lend themselves to the projection of sexual symbolization.[3] Other flyers attach hostile, aggressive fantasies to flight. (See section on hostility and aggression in flying dreams later in this chapter.)

Most air passengers automatically repress any sexual fantasies which they may have during flight. The phobic flyer cannot contain his anxiety by simple repression. As described earlier, he also *projects* his conflict outward and *displaces* it onto some innocuous aspects of the external situation. (See list of fears in Chapter 2.) Taking a flight is inherently an assertive act. If a flyer has strong internal prohibitions against self-assertion, his irrational conscience may punish him for flying as if he had actually committed a crime. It will also convert potentially pleasurable feelings into painful ones. You probably have recognized that this self-punishment for having asserted oneself lies at the basis of the myths discussed earlier in this chapter.

There is no reason to suppose that phobic flyers have greater separation anxieties or more guilt feelings than do other flyers. As we saw in Chapter 2, they are not more "neurotic" than most people. In fact, they frequently function more effectively than the average person. Obviously, additional ingredients must be present to account for the phobic behavior of the fearful flyer.

3. *The phobic flyer attaches basic fears to flight.* Anybody who has been in an air accident or even read about one will become temporarily fearful about flying. Ordinarily, however, he will not be dissuaded from ever flying

[3] See Leon J. Saul and Burton A. Fleming, "A Clinical Note on the Ego Meaning of Certain Dreams of Flying," *Psychoanalytic Quarterly*, IV (1959), 501–504. Also see Douglas D. Bond, *The Love and the Fear of Flying* (New York: International University Press, 1952).

again. We all know that more than 55,000 Americans are killed each year on the highways, yet most of us do not give up driving. Something in the life history of the phobic flyer causes him to attach basic conflicts onto flight. How this comes about can only be ascertained by an exploration of the flyer's personal history. Certain techniques to ascertain why a particular person attaches core conflicts to flying will be described in chapters 6, 7, and 8.

4. Another essential component of the fear of flying is *fear of loss of control*. Ambitious, hard-driving, successful people (precisely the type of person I described in Chapter 1) are particularly likely to become anxious if they do not have things under control. These individuals abhor the passive role of an airline passenger. They become fearful and angry in the flight situation because it requires that they be immobilized, fly on someone else's schedule and depend totally on strangers. Some passengers, in this condition of enforced passivity (so unlike the total freedom portrayed in dreams and fantasies of flying), develop marked emotional reactions to the airline, pilot, stewardesses, adjacent passengers, and even to the entire group of passengers. (Some of these reactions were described in Chapter 2.) Since they have little opportunity to test the reality of these perceptions or to discharge their feelings appropriately, tensions accumulate and increase their susceptibility to phobic reactions to flight. In addition to having to control the outside world, this type of passenger frequently has a strong need to control his own anxiety. In a sense, he is allergic to his anxiety. Even slight increases in the amount of anxiety he experiences threaten his image of himself as a person who is always in charge.

5. *The phobic flyer may fear the consequences of flying.* Some phobic flyers are not basically afraid of flying per se. Rather, they fear flying will bring about unforeseen changes in their relationships to people close to them or will disrupt their way of life. This is particularly true in certain marital relationships. If husband and wife are both afraid to fly,

fear of flying does not ordinarily constitute an acute problem. However, if one mate is fearful and the other is not, latent marital conflicts may become aggravated. Not infrequently one mate *uses* the phobia to control the spouse.

For example, some wives become extremely critical if their husbands are not active or assertive. Instead of accepting their husband's fears, they urge them to push ahead no matter what the consequences. If the husband has a flying phobia or other fears of self-assertion, he may perceive his wife as forcing him into a situation that could prove dangerous or even fatal. The husband may, in retaliation, use his fear of flying to frustrate his wife. He may say, in effect, "I would like to please you, to succeed, to be successful, to 'fly high,' but there is nothing I can do about it because I have this irrational fear."

Similarly, wives who fear, resent, or envy their husbands' assertiveness may use their phobias to prevent their husbands from flying. (See the case of Mary below.)

GUILT AND PUNISHMENT IN FLYING DREAMS

Following is a dream illustrating how flying may be perceived unconsciously as dangerous, even if the dreamer has no conscious fear of flying.

"I was in a plane that was shaped like the caterpillar ride you sometimes see in an amusement park. It was careening through space at a breakneck speed of thousands of miles an hour. It seemed to be going as fast as a comet. It did not go in a straight line, but flew up and down erratically. I was terrified because I had the feeling that the plane was being piloted by a lunatic. Although I was not afraid of an imminent crash I felt panicky because I didn't know what the pilot's next move would be."

At the time he told me this dream the patient was extremely fearful that his own impulses, which were coming closer to the surface in psychotherapy, would become completely uncontrollable. The plane "careening through space at a breakneck speed" represents his own impulses. In this phase of his therapy he was dealing with his childhood fear of an irrational, violent, uncontrollable father. His father (as well as the father in himself) is represented by the "lunatic pilot." The dream reflects the dreamer's ambition to have unlimited power. It also indicates his terror of being punished by his father for wanting such power. As mentioned above, this patient had no fear of flying.

The following dream, by contrast, is by a male patient who was terrified of flying but was totally unable to describe his fears in words. His dream yields some valuable clues.

"I was in an airplane with a group of people. The plane crashed in an open field. As we all got out of the plane we were herded together in the field. Suddenly soldiers came out of nowhere and machine-gunned us. Everyone was killed but myself."

This dream proved extremely helpful in working with the patient. It revealed that he was not afraid of a plane crash at all. (As you can see, nobody was hurt in the plane crash itself.) His real fear was what would happen *after* he reached his destination.

Some weeks prior to the dream, he had been offered a promotion to a job which necessitated a great deal of flying. His fear was that if he flew (and, as a result, got the promotion) he would become hemmed in by the restrictions of corporate life ("herded together") and would end up a "prisoner." Paradoxically, in his mind, flying meant less freedom rather than more.

The following dream by a female patient is an example of how flying, aggression and sexuality may merge at the unconscious level.

"I heard gunshots in my room. I saw Indians shooting arrows at me. I began to dig at the base of a wall in much the same way a dog digs to get under a fence, but to no avail. Then I lifted myself up. My body was still and I was lying on my back, face upward, with my arms stretched out. As I moved my arms, I flew higher and faster. The sensation of flight was wonderful. And then, suddenly, I separated my legs and stopped flying. I was disappointed that it lasted only a few seconds and I could not understand why when I separated my legs I stopped flying."

This dream contains a disguised reference to masturbation—"flying alone." Its content indicates that the dreamer is too guilt-ridden to allow herself to derive pleasure from masturbation. It is interesting to note that during periods of extreme tension she would engage in impulsive flights to nearby cities. At these times she would behave promiscuously with strangers. Her promiscuity and impulsive flying both had an identical meaning: They represented desperate attempts to achieve sexual gratification.

HOSTILITY AND AGGRESSION IN FLYING DREAMS

The following dream shows vividly how flying and hostility may become unconsciously connected:

"At various times in the dream my entire family came into focus, but never my wife. These airplanes just crashed one after another. Some of the bystanders were hurt or afraid of the closeness of the crashes. At times I attempted to help the victims of the crashes. At other times I just didn't care and wished it would get worse. As far as I can remember I was never in the crashing plane but almost felt exhilaration at the fury and destruction caused by the crashes."

The crashing planes represent the dreamer's hostility. He is openly aware of the pleasure he derives from venting his destructive impulses. (Usually this degree of sadism is more disguised in dreams.)

Another dream illustrating a connection between hostility and flying is the following:

"I am strafed by enemy planes. The enemy is unknown

and the war, for me, serves no purpose. I wake up just before I die."

In this dream the patient sees himself as the target of hostility. The reasons for this are unclear.

"I dreamed that I was a spectator at some kind of airplane contest. The airplanes were racing not far above the ground. There was a solid wall. One plane zoomed over the wall. Another crashed through the wall and there was an ugly hole in it. The latter plane burst into flames. The pilot died and so did his companion, a flamboyant young woman. I remember thinking to myself that it was fortunate that the old pilot was killed instead of the younger one."

The dream expresses death wishes toward the patient's father (old men or older men in dreams usually represent father figures). "Crashing into the wall" suggests that he regards sex as a violent act.

The following dream is by a female teenage patient:

"President Nixon declared that we had bombed Cambodia. He was going to accelerate the war and he needed more pilots. He was going around to each college to pick the best people. He picked my boy friend, John. John ended up in a plane but did not fly it or drop the bombs. He was shot down. He was not killed but ended up in some sort of jungle."

This patient, a pacifist, is consciously opposed to any form of aggression. However, in this dream she expresses unconscious hostility toward her boy friend. She allows him to be shot down but is too guilty to let him die. President Nixon represents her father. She is overly attached to her father and cannot allow herself to get involved with other males at this stage of her life.

Following are a series of dreams of two patients with whom I had the opportunity to explore in depth the fear of flying over a period of several months. Both had marked flying phobias. As you will see, flying reactivated basic conflicts in both of them. Notice how certain themes emerge and develop in the dream series of each patient.

THE CASE OF MARY

Mary had developed an acute fear of flying approximately one year before coming to see me. She had had some previous therapy for other problems. Since she was unusually frank and insightful, we were able to get to the roots of her flying phobia relatively quickly.

I. "I was in a plane. It was on the ground. There were a lot of people on the plane, a lot of confusion. The passengers were predominantly men. I had the feeling that this was a business flight. The plane was taxiing. Everyone was up out of his seat and there was a lot of confusion. The plane stopped and the stewardess said they had to unload the whole plane. I don't know whether there were too many people or too much luggage or something, but the plane wasn't going to take off. I don't know if I was disappointed or relieved or both, but that was the end of it. The plane never got off the ground."

Associating to this dream, Mary said, "I'd like to be able to go on a business flight myself. I think I envy people who are on business and do things and go places." Mary indicated in further associations to this dream that she would have liked to have been born a male so that she could "do things and go places like men." The stewardess who interrupts the flight turned out, upon further questioning, to represent her mother. Mary always felt that her mother discouraged her self-assertiveness. Unconsciously, Mary equated assertiveness with maleness and non-assertiveness with being female.

II. "I was in a big house in the country. I wasn't me. I was a man. I was boyish-looking and young and I was carrying a gun, a rifle or a shotgun—probably a shotgun. I could not get it to shoot. Someone else—a man—took it and fired it. When I tried to fire it, it only made a click. I kept pointing the muzzle down to the ground with the idea that I did not want it to hurt anyone. I was afraid to point it at the ground because I thought if it did go off while it was pointed down, I would get hurt. When I tried to fire it, it just went 'click.' I felt it was dangerous because it was armed, but it did not go off."

In this dream, which she had one week after the first dream, Mary portrays again her wish to be male. She also indicates that she sees men as sexually violent. When she identifies with men, her own aggression is activated. This frightens her.

III. "A small man, but physically well developed, was locked up in a room. It was small and part of it was a bathroom. It was very dirty. There were cigarette butts all over the place. He tried to open the back door. It was a screen door and it just opened. He ran out and there were people chasing him. He started to swing through the air on a vine—a regular Tarzan routine—at which point he suddenly lost his drawers. [Laughs] He meets up with this lady who was swinging on a trapeze. She is angry because she did not want him on her trapeze. This green foliage, which I hate, was all over the place. It is usually full of bugs and is very humid." (As a child, Mary had phobic fears of insects.)

In this dream, Mary expresses a deprecatory attitude toward the aggressively male figure on the vine. Again, she reveals resentment at the idea that men have more power than women. There are also indications in this dream, as well as in her case history, that she perceives the sexual act as "dirty."

IV. "I was at an airport. I was supposed to go to Boston. There was a woman there, an older woman. I could not get on the plane. There was some moment of indecision, but I finally decided, without hysterics, "I am not going to get on this plane. I am too afraid."

The older woman is her mother. You will recall in an earlier dream that it was a stewardess who stopped the flight. Here it is an older woman. Both symbolize her mother. Mary feels that her mother does not want her to fly, to be a male. At the same time she cannot accept her own femininity. As a result, she is in a state of indecision as to her sexual identity.

V. "I was able to fly by myself. It was more of a floating feeling than actually flying. I was looking out of a high window—probably eight to sixteen stories high. (The author's office is on the eighth floor.) So I got out the window and floated, sort of. And then it dawned on me that the only reason I could fly was because I thought I could and that if I began to think that I could not, I would fall. I was sort of losing power and I began to go down but I didn't crash down, I floated down. There was something about me that could not be hurt. I was invincible! I had the feeling I was performing this act of flying for a woman—an older woman who emanated a feeling of comfort and warmth."

Mary had this dream the night *before* her first successful flight. Apparently, she had temporarily projected a good-mother image onto the male therapist and wanted to please him by flying.

VI. "I dreamt the entire flight from beginning to end in complete detail. It was one of the most realistic dreams I ever had. We got onto the plane. It was a normal plane. I don't remember taking off specifically but we did. We flew and we landed and it was all right. My husband was with me."

This dream took place the night *after* Mary's first successful flight. It reveals that she has achieved good mastery of her flying fears (although she still avoids the take-off) and suggests an improvement in her relationship with her husband.

THE CASE OF JAMES

James's personality is typical of the men described in Chapter 1. He is a highly successful, perfectionistic man with a very strong conscience who does not allow himself many outlets for his feelings. Though somewhat depressed in demeanor, he is very active and generally functions quite well. He has an extremely marked fear of flying.

I. "The plane has crashed. I am trying to help get the people off. I am particularly trying to get my family off the plane but am unable to do so."

James shows, in this dream, his characteristic concern for the welfare of others. He always gives the impression of carrying the cares of the world on his shoulders. This dream represents an unconscious wish to lighten his burden, to be rid of his family. Naturally, such a thought is unacceptable to his conscience.

II. "I was going on a vacation with my wife on a plane. It seemed like everything went very well. I never actually got on the plane or off the plane but we did get to where we wanted to go by plane and there wasn't much of a problem."

James is expressing a wish to have a happy relationship with his wife. Since the idea of flying is so painful to him, he obliterates the actual flight, but somehow manages to get to his destination.

III. "I have to go somewhere alone and I am very afraid. I envision the plane taking off vertically—the way an astronaut takes off. I realize I have gone through this dream many times before—seeing the plane take off and then burning and coming down. I don't know when I dreamed about it, whether it was when I was two years old or five years old. But it seemed to come back to me that I was dreaming about this quite a bit. The plane seemed to be a fiery wreck coming to the ground."

James is consciously afraid of a plane explosion. My guess is that this explosion represents symbolically a sexual orgasm, an anger explosion or possibly both. James is extremely reserved and is fearful of all strong feelings, sexual as well as aggressive. Essentially he is phobophobic.

IV. "We were either on a plane or a train. I don't remember which. My wife was sitting next to me. You [the therapist] were there. My friend John was there with two girls. At that point I seemed to become very possessive with my wife. I brought her over to sit next to me. It ends up with the girls starting to suggest a particular orgy or something. A sexual part gets into it and I get up and I am ready to leave at that point together with my wife."

In this dream James is expressing envy of his friend's extramarital relationships. He too is tempted, but his strong conscience requires him to remove himself from the situation. His leaving with his wife is, in my opinion, not solely a matter of conscience; it also reflects his very strong dependency on her.

V. "I was coming home from a business meeting. I was sidetracked on the way home by a girl. I continued running home very fast. I found myself trying to lift my legs to get off the ground. Finally, I was running so fast I was almost flying. There was no plane. I was just by myself. I finally got to my house. I shouted my wife's name when I got there."

Again, James is struggling with fantasies of infidelity. He is tempted but feels too guilty. Also, he is fearful of being able to survive as an independent person if he leaves home.

VI. "I get under a car and fix it. I hold a torch underneath the car. It explodes."

The car represents himself. He is afraid that if he examines himself too closely in therapy he will explode. In a sense, he is afraid to "light his own fire."

VII. "I was in bed with my wife and another girl. The three of us were having an orgy. Everything seemed rather normal. We started to go to a room where there was music and dancing. A man on the stage was dressed in black. I was dancing around the room with this girl. I had a tremendous feeling of freedom. I was screaming and yelling with delight. As we came to the end of the dancing, I slid across the floor. *It was something like flying* across the floor. Later, I was told that somebody had just smacked a car up completely and was dead. I could picture the accident near the house where I grew up. I acted as if I did not care what happened. The man on the stage went into tremendous laughter."

James is again expressing his impulse to have extramarital relations. "Dancing" and "sliding along the floor" are symbols of sexual intercourse. The "man in black" is his irrational conscience. The smash-up of the car represents self-punishment for sexual and extramarital impulses.

James's problem is more complicated than Mary's. She is primarily struggling with problems of sexual identification and is engaged in a power struggle with her husband. James, by contrast, is in conflict over (1) sexual guilts, (2) dependency needs (separation anxiety), (3) fear of his own hostility, (4) extramarital fantasies, and (5) fear of *all* strong feelings (phobophobia).

THE USE OF DRAWINGS TO STUDY THE FEAR OF FLYING

I have found drawings extremely valuable in arriving at an understanding of what flying means to the individual. First, I ask each fearful flyer to visualize taking a trip on a commercial airliner. Then I ask him to portray the most pleasurable aspects of flying he can imagine. In a second drawing I ask him to portray the most unpleasant consequences he can imagine. The material that emerges in these drawings frequently is quite a revelation to the drawer. It yields important clues as to which needs he wishes to fulfill by flying and what punishments he anticipates from his irrational conscience.

I would like to suggest that you render these two drawings yourself before reading further. Do them as quickly as possible. Artistic skill is of no consequence here. The important thing is to get a pictorial representation of your wishes and fears of flying.

Following is a summary of the content of a series of

"most pleasant drawings" which I collected from fearful flyers as well as from patients who came to me for other problems. In some cases the needs expressed in these drawings are patently obvious. In other cases they are more obscure. I will indicate in parentheses my guesses as to which needs are being expressed. It might be interesting for you to compare your guesses with mine.

"Most Pleasant" Drawings

Lying on a couch in the sun (sensual pleasure).

Walking in an open field with a dog (freedom, nonconfinement).

A sexual situation entitled "Orgasm and Joy" (meaning obvious).

Being surrounded by one's entire family and being very happy with them (belonging to a happy family).

Flying through the skies with a feeling of openness and speed (freedom, power, possibly sexuality).

Being outdoors in the sun with a lot of friendly people (sensuality, group belongingness).

Being on a ship with husband and child while a waiter brings a meal in an elegant setting (improved marital relationship, being taken care of).

Opening a door lock with a key (understanding, sexuality).

Flying on a large plane with a group of people (belong to a congenial group).

Being at an outdoor pool with a group of people. The sun is shining and there are mountains in the background (belong to a congenial group).

A house on a hilltop in Italy (secure home).

A house entitled "Home, Sweet Home" (secure home life).

Lying on a beach with an umbrella nearby, the sun shining overhead (sensual pleasure).

A man and woman are standing outside a house. A very peaceful setting (security and sexuality).

A woman dancing by herself with a feeling of freedom (self-expression, freedom).

A man is standing by himself with two chains on his hands. One chain is labeled "Health, Happiness and Youth"; the other is entitled "Phobias, Fears, Anxieties, Illness." Both chains are broken (escape from anxiety).

A man and a woman on a tropical island. The sun is shining (sensual pleasure).

A man is lying in the sun in a Caribbean setting (sensual pleasure).

Picture of the drawer's son (to be closer to son).

A man and a woman are embracing each other in a movie house as they watch a film together (closeness, sensual pleasure).

A woman is sitting in a tropical setting under a palm tree. The sun is shining overhead (sensual pleasure).

A man is playing golf alone on a golf course (freedom, sexual potency).

A woman and several of her female companions enter a plane. There is a tree nearby (closeness with females).

Three smiling people. The drawing is entitled "To Be with Friends" (meaning obvious).

Two people are sitting in front of a fireplace in a cozy house while a blizzard rages outside (security, closeness).

A woman is fantasizing that she is lying in the sun on a beach near the ocean (sensual pleasure).

A plane is flying through the sky. There are clouds and sunshine (freedom, power).

A man is being served by a stewardess. He is holding a drink of liquor in his hand (nurturing mother).

A plane is parked on the ground. The landing gear is down and the ladder entering the plane is set in place. People are getting on the plane. The picture is entitled "Going to a Pleasant and Nice Place" (meaning obvious).

A man is on a tropical beach. There are palm trees and coconuts. The sun is shining (sensual pleasure, freedom).

A man and a woman are seated next to each other on a

plane. Music is playing and the mood is pleasant. The title of this drawing is "Honeymoon Special" (meaning obvious).

A control panel of an "intergalactic vehicle." The title of the drawing is "Going at the Speed of Light" (power, freedom).

A man is flying on a plane. He is being served by a hostess (nurture, being taken care of).

A man is flying through the skies. His friends are waving him off (freedom, power, friendship).

Large spaceship flying through the sky (power, freedom).

A woman is sitting in a plane holding a glass of liquor in her hand (nurture, being taken care of).

A plane is flying through the air. The sun is shining. There are palm trees and a blue lagoon (freedom and sensuality).

A man and a woman are on a plane. The man has his arms around the woman (closeness, sensuality).

A woman is on a plane looking out the window (exploration).

A woman is flying about in a room (freedom, power).

A man and a woman are seated at a table on a plane watching a film. The sun is shining outside. The woman has a crown on her head. The man has a beard (sensuality, closeness, power).

A spaceship is flying through space (freedom, power).

A woman is seated on a plane. She and a man have their arms around each other. The sun is shining. Soothing music is playing (closeness, sensuality).

A passenger is looking through a window of a plane. The plane is in the midst of white fleecy clouds (freedom, detachment).

"Most Unpleasant" Drawings

I would like now to summarize some of the "most unpleasant" drawings drawn for me by phobic flyers. I shall indicate in parentheses which phobia seems to be expressed in each drawing (see Chapter 4).

A man is walking on a tightrope (acrophobia).

A woman is lying alone in a hospital bed (illness).

A man is behind bars in a jail (claustrophobia).

No drawings, but a written comment, "A member of my family is ill or has died" (illness, death).

A figure is encased in a small cell-like room with a black area all around. A very lonely, desolate feeling (claustrophobia).

Four men are being herded together in a prison camp by a man carrying a machine gun (physical harm).

In a physician's office. The physician is saying, "I am sorry, but it is malignant!" The woman is grief-stricken (cancerphobia).

A tombstone with dates written on it (death).

A woman is in a cemetery looking at four tombstones, each of which is inscribed with names of members of her family (death).

A tombstone entitled "Here lies James R.I.P." (death).

No drawing. Only the word "anxiety" (phobophobia).

No drawing. Entitled "In a Hospital or Suffering" (illness).

A plane is breaking in two in mid-air (death).

A woman in a cell (claustrophobia).

A plane is crashing into a mountaintop in a tropical setting. The sun is shining (acrophobia).

A man is stranded on top of a high mountain surrounded by other mountains. Presumably, he will not be able to get down (acrophobia).

A woman is buried in a ditch by a man with a shovel (claustrophobia).

A group of people are sitting, tightly confined in a compartment (claustrophobia).

A person is by herself. The title of the drawing is "Most Frightening Is to Be Isolated from People" (being alone).

Three people are sitting in a rectangular-shaped subway

train. The title of the picture is "Caught in a Subway Train That Is Not Moving" (claustrophobia).

A woman is struck by a bolt of lightning. There is a tree on the ground and clouds overhead (astrophobia).

A woman is all by herself (being alone).

Please review some of the ideas expressed in this chapter in relation to your own fears of flying. Try to establish connections between your flying fears and any other phobic reactions you may have. Once you grasp the concept that your fear of flying is an outward manifestation of inner conflicts, you can begin to "desymbolize" your concept of flying. This should help you diminish your anxiety on your next flight. Also, having arrived at the realization that fear of flying is not the real issue, you might be motivated to take a closer look at yourself and see how the same factors underlying your fear of flying may be causing difficulties in other aspects of your life.

Try, as I suggested earlier, to recall dreams of flying. It is almost a rule of thumb that a dream containing the theme of flying will give you clues as to what is causing your fears.

We know from practical experience that it is entirely possible for you to overcome or at least to suppress your fears of flying without getting to root causes. The next chapter will discuss certain ways of dealing with fears of flying which do not require "deep" insight. However, there is no question that partial insight can accelerate your efforts to overcome the flying phobia.

In the meantime, ask yourself these questions:

1. How do I characteristically react to changes in familiar surroundings?

2. How do I inhibit impulses to assert myself?

3. How do I regard flight symbolically?

4. How do I handle my strong feelings?

5. How do I imagine my intimate relationships will be altered if I fly?

PART II

CHAPTER 6

How to Help Yourself
Overcome the Fear
of Flying

IN THIS CHAPTER I shall recommend certain steps you can take on your own to overcome the fear of flying. These steps have helped many fearful flyers. They should help you, particularly if your fears are relatively mild. Even if you have a full-fledged flying phobia, some of the ideas in this chapter should prove useful. I plan to:

1. Outline certain techniques to help you determine why you are afraid to fly.

2. Suggest ways to diminish your anxiety.

3. Help you to achieve mastery by suggesting specific actions before and during a flight.

HOW TO DETERMINE WHICH NEEDS AND FEARS YOU HAVE ATTACHED TO FLYING

Here are some steps you can take to determine, at least partially, why you are afraid to fly. Some of these have been mentioned earlier in the book. *This time, follow them systematically!*

1. List all the reasons you want to fly. Try to go beyond the obvious. Remember, many people are quite content not to fly or to fly only rarely.

2. Describe your fears exactly in writing. Compare your fears with those listed in Chapter 2.

3. Rank these fears. Which is the *most* frightening? Which is the *least?* Determine if these fears fall into clusters. If so, what theme seems to underlie each cluster?

4. On separate pages write the following words: *plane, flight, crash.* List, in rank order, the fears you have about each. After you have done this, write down five or more words that come to mind when you think of each of these words. Do not censor! Just write down the first words that occur to you. This will further help you to determine what it is that you really fear.

5. Imagine yourself taking a flight. Render two drawings. In the first drawing portray the most pleasant characteristics you can think of in connection with flight. In the second drawing indicate the most unpleasant things you can imagine in relation to flight. Compare your drawings to those summarized in Chapter 5. Remember, artistic skill is of no relevance here. The main purpose is to obtain a pictorial representation of your needs, guilts and fears, uninfluenced by words.

6. Write out any daydreams you have ever had about flying, either flying your own plane or being a passenger on a commercial airline. Read what you have written and see what ideas occur to you. These daydreams should yield valuable leads as to the wishes and fears you have attached to flying.

7. Do the same for dreams of flying. Recurrent dreams of flying are especially valuable for this purpose. Dreams tap deeper levels than are ordinarily reached by daydreams.

If you cannot recall any dreams of flying, do the following: (1) Consciously instruct yourself to have one just before going to sleep. (Suspend any doubts about the impossibility of "dreaming to order.") (2) Keep a pencil and paper next to your bed. (3) Lie perfectly still upon awakening. Gaze for a while at a wall or the ceiling of your room. Avoid moving your head while doing so. (4) As soon as the visual image of the dream appears, write it down. (5) If you have difficulty in understanding a dream, read a *scientific* book on dream symbols and mechanisms—for example, Sigmund Freud's *The Interpretation of Dreams* and Emil Gutheil's *The Handbook of Dream Analysis*. This will help you decipher the dream.

8. Select one dream of flying, preferably a recurrent one. Make believe the dream events are actually taking place in the present. Write a script for each person or object in the dream and act it out. For examples: "I am a big plane—I am hurtling through space. . . . I am the captain of the plane—I control its movements. . . . I am a frightened passenger—I am holding tightly onto my seat. . . ."

Try to determine which symbols (objects or people) represent your inner needs. Which represent your healthy executive self? Also, which represent your irrational conscience? Arrange an imaginary dialogue between your inner needs, your healthy self, and your irrational conscience. Do battle with your irrational conscience! Defeat its attempts to gain ascendancy over your healthy self.

The rationale here is as follows: All characters and objects in your dreams are really projections of parts of yourself. By playing out these roles you gain insight into the internal conflicts you characteristically project while flying; you also reassimilate some of these projections into yourself.[1]

PSYCHOLOGICAL EXERCISES TO INCREASE YOUR MASTERY OF THE FLYING FEAR

As I mentioned in Chapter 5, the enforced passivity inherent in the role of an airline passenger induces feelings of powerlessness and generates anxieties in many flyers.

[1] For further discussion of this rationale, read Frederick A. Perls, *Gestalt Theory Verbatim* (Lafayette, Calif.: Real People Press, 1969).

Any technique which gives one a feeling that one is not completely at the mercy of external forces will reduce his anxiety.

Here are some psychological exercises to help you gain mastery over your anxiety.[2]

1. While lying down or seated comfortably on a chair, visualize all sensations and anxieties you experience while on a plane. Simply visualizing yourself on a plane may make you anxious at first. You may find yourself wanting to avoid thinking about it. If so, let your mind dwell on pleasant thoughts for a while. As soon as you feel somewhat more relaxed, reenter the fantasy of being anxious on a plane. Focus initially on the least frightening aspects of flight. Gradually allow yourself to visualize more frightening fears. Each time you practice this exercise you will be able to get closer to the dangerous situation and stay with it longer. Do this exercise twice a day for a week.

2. During an actual flight try the following exercise: Picture yourself in the *most pleasant* situation you can imagine. Let your mind dwell on this pleasant situation as long as possible. When you return to the realistically unpleasant situation—namely, being on a plane—some of the positive feelings you experienced in your fantasy will come back with you and help allay your anxiety.

3. There is another useful exercise to try while aboard a plane: Visualize the *most unpleasant* situation you can possibly think of—a situation *even more unpleasant to you than being on a plane!* You will find when you leave this fantasy and return to the reality of flying, you will experience less anxiety than you did while having the fantasy!

4. Read the following exercise recommended by G. Donald MacClean and Robert W. Graff in "Behavioral Bibliotherapy: A Simple Home Remedy for Fears" and adapt it to your specific fears of flying:

[2] Other exercises in the same vein may be found *ibid.*

In many cases, when you have a specific kind of fear or anxiety, such as test anxiety or speech anxiety, a crucially important part of the fear is a wish to avoid or escape from the feared situation. As long as the wish persists, reciprocally the fear will persist. If you can persuade yourself to experience that fear without trying to avoid it, the vicious circle of fear leading to the escape urge leading to more fear can be unwound. (The footsteps that follow you past a cemetery in the dark become louder and more menacing the more you hurry. Only when you stop and permit them to approach do they disappear.)

The home remedy for fear is simply to experience the fear, deliberately and as fully as possible. The technique is probably most efficient if you have a sympathetic friend present so you can verbalize and act out the fear. Think about the feared situation or object. Imagine that you are in the feared situation, or actually put yourself in the feared situation. In some cases it may be easier to do this in progressive stages. As you do so, do not attend primarily to the feared situation or to the wish to escape the situation. Concentrate on the fear itself. Attend as actively as you can and experience as fully as you can the unpleasant emotions and all the concomitant bodily sensations that are aroused. It it's appropriate, go on to imagine all the undesirable consequences of being in the feared situation, the failure and loss of self-esteem that will result, and the ensuing scorn, ridicule, and rejection by friends, parents, and others.

Take, for example, an agoraphobic person, anyone who cannot walk from home to his place of work alone· He might begin by going to the foot of his front doo' steps, where he experiences all the fear possible there. When he has tried and tried to feel all the fear possible and becomes so bored by it that he cannot feel more, then he advances, say, twenty-five steps or so down the sidewalk, or until the fear is rekindled. There again he is to stand still and experience his emotion, and so on.

It is very important for you to understand that the aim of the exercises is to experience the fears and all the bodily sensations that always accompany them and not simply to achieve such and such a distance, or such and such a contact. One often meets people, particularly people with phobias of situations rather than objects (situations are less easily avoided), who say they can do so and so if they have to; but the mere doing of it does not at all reduce the phobic abhorrence the next time. Facing a feared situation by sheer will power is possible in many cases, but this does nothing to reduce the fear. *For successful fear reduction, full attention to and experience of the internal unpleasantness is essential.*

In some cases where it is more convenient to imagine the feared situation, it may be necessary to repeat the treatment a number of times. Say you are suffering from test anxiety and you use this method to reduce the fear. You may do so at a time when you are not faced with a test. As the date of an actual examination approaches, you may begin to experience some fear. Do two things. First, every time you feel a little wave of spontaneous alarm, do not push it aside. Enhance it, augment, try to experience it more profoundly and more vividly. Second, if you do not spontaneously feel fear, make a special, deliberate effort to try to do so two or three or six times a day, no matter how difficult or ludicrous this might seem.

This technique works best with specific fears. The more specific the fear, the more effective the technique. It works best if there is a sympathetic friend present, to whom you can describe your sensations as you experience your fear. Like most good home remedies, it sometimes doesn't work at all, but it can cause little harm, and sometimes it works amazingly well.[3]

5. Try the following relaxing exercises recommended by Dr. Lewis R. Wolberg, dean of the Postgraduate Center for Mental Health:

[3] G. Donald MacClean and Robert W. Graff, "Behavioral Bibliotherapy: A Simple Home Remedy for Fears," *Psychotherapy,* VII (1970), 118–119.

These exercises may be performed the first thing in the morning before getting out of bed. They may be repeated during the day if desired. They should always be done at night prior to retiring; relaxing suggestions will eventually merge into sleep.

The total time for each session should be at least twenty minutes.

After shutting your eyes, proceed with the following steps:

1. Deep slow breathing for about ten breaths.

2. Progressive muscle relaxation from forehead, face, neck, to finger tips; from chest to toes, visualizing and purposefully loosening each muscle group.

3. Visualize a wonderfully relaxed scene or simply a blank white wall.

4. Slow counting to self from 1 to 20 while visualizing the relaxed scene (or white wall).

5. Relaxing or sleeping from one to two minutes during which visualization of the relaxed scene continues.

6. Make the following suggestions to yourself (using the word "you"):

a. *Symptom relief* (disturbing symptoms, like tension, etc., will get less and less upsetting).

b. *Self-confidence* (self-assuredness will grow).

c. *Situational control* (visualize impending difficult situations and successful mastery of them).

d. *Self-understanding* (make connections if possible between flareups of symptoms and precipitating events and inner conflicts).

7. Relax or sleep for several more minutes.

8. During daytime arouse yourself by counting from 1 to 5.

At night do not arouse yourself; continue relaxing until sleep supervenes.

If sleep begins developing during the 4th step before the count comes to an end, interrupt counting and proceed immediately to suggestions (6th step above). Then continue with count and go as deeply as you wish. A racing of the mind and a tendency to distraction are normal. When this occurs force your attention back to exercises.

Remember, you will not really be asleep during these exercises. You will be aware of your thoughts and of stimuli on the outside. If, for any reason, before you finish you want to bring yourself out of the relaxed state, tell yourself that at the count of 5 you will be out of it. Count from 1 to 5 and say to yourself: "Be wide awake now, open your eyes." If negative thoughts crop up, bypass them, and continue with the steps outlined above. Results are rarely immediate. It takes a while to neutralize negative suggestions you have been giving yourself all your life. So be patient. Persistence is the keynote to success.[4]

ACHIEVING MASTERY BY LEARNING MORE ABOUT FLYING

One way to gain mastery of an unfamiliar situation is to learn as much as you can about it. To learn more about flying, take the following steps:

1. Reread Chapter 3 of this book ("Realistic Aspects of Commercial Flight").

2. Read the material on commercial aviation in the "Selected References" at the conclusion of this book.

3. Ask your travel agent or nearest airline office to send you any available information on commercial flight. Many airlines publish excellent brochures on such matters as what makes a plane fly, pilot training, safety procedures and the like.

4. Ask your librarian to recommend books on commercial aviation. You will be amazed at how many such books exist.

5. If you would like to learn more about the activities

[4] Lewis R. Wolberg, *The Technique of Psychotherapy* (New York: Grune & Stratton, 1967), II, 1295. Reprinted by permission of Dr. Wolberg and Grune & Stratton, Inc.

of the Federal Aviation Administration, write to Library Services Division, Federal Aviation Administration, Department of Transportation, Washington, D.C. 20590. A bibliography of over-all aviation facts and figures entitled *Aviation Education Bibliography,* edited by Jane R. Marshall, may be obtained from the National Aerospace Educational Council, 806 15th Street, N.W., Washington, D.C. 20005, 50 cents.

If you are interested in studying the causes of air accidents, write to the Bureau of Aviation Safety, National Transportation Safety Board, Washington, D.C. 20591, or read Robert J. Serling's *Loud and Clear,* Dell Publishing, New York, 1970 (paperback).

For highly informative material on all aspects of commercial aviation, write to the Air Transport Association, 100 Connecticut Avenue, N.W., Washington, D.C. 20036. Ask especially for their pamphlet entitled "How Safe Is Flying?" Also, if you have never flown, request the pamphlet "How to Fly."

6. Follow news developments on commercial aviation in your local newspaper. I have personally found *The New York Times* extremely helpful in this respect. The *Times* gives frequent coverage of new developments in commercial air travel.

7. Aviation publications of interest are: *Aviation Daily, Airline Management and Marketing, Air Transport World, Space/Aeronautics and Air Travel.*

8. Contact the directors of public relations (or equivalent title) of the major airlines in your city. (If you live in a small town, you may have to contact airline officials in the nearest large city.) These officials will be pleased to answer any questions you have about flying or refer you to someone who can. It may even be possible for you or a group of other fearful flyers to arrange to meet personally with airline personnel who will answer factual questions about flying.

The airlines are increasingly aware of the need to help

people overcome their fears of flying and are most co-operative in this respect. Their representatives will treat you with great courtesy. In addition to benefiting from the valuable factual information they provide, you will be very reassured by meeting the people involved in airlines operations. These professionals, in my experience, convey an aura of competence which will make you feel more inclined to trust your safety to the airlines.

9. Take a trip to a major airport alone or, preferably, with friends who understand and accept your fear of flying. Watch the hundreds of planes which arrive and depart every day. Even if you remain skeptical of safety statistics, seeing is believing. Observing thousands of people arrive and depart safely each hour can be very reassuring.

A number of fearful flyers whom I know benefited greatly by visiting airports in congenial groups. While having a drink or two in the airport lounge, they were able to observe dozens of planes take off and land. By taking this step, they provided invaluable support to each other. They also partially desensitized themselves by getting closer to planes.

I want to caution you against spending *too* much time obtaining information about flying. One obvious drawback is that this can become very time-consuming. Much more important is the danger that you may unduly delay taking a flight. You do not have to be an aviation expert to fly with pleasure! Try not to become overly compulsive and preoccupied with the fine points of flying. Begin to take action!

ACHIEVING MASTERY BY TAKING ACTION PRIOR TO FLYING

Take the following actions prior to embarking on a flight. They will increase your confidence. They will also reduce feelings of being unable to control your destiny.

1. Choose a travel agent who is not only knowledgeable but who can devote attention to your personal needs. Ask him to specify what types of planes go to your destination. Also, ask him to describe these planes with regard to seating capacity, comfort, speed, etc. If you are going to a popular destination, the chances are you will have a choice of several airlines and types of plane.

Here are some other ways a good travel agent can facilitate air travel, eliminating unnecessary wear and tear on yourself: [5]

A travel agent not only will suggest where you might like to travel and how much it will cost, but will take care of all the arrangements for your trip. He can arrange transportation, whether by air, ship, bus, rail or car, or in any combination.

He can book you into a group tour, a personally escorted tour, or a special interest tour, or he can prepare an itinerary fitting your individual needs and interests.

He can arrange for your hotel, motel, or resort accommodations, meals, sightseeing, transfers between rail and air terminals and hotels. He can get you tickets for plays, operas, and concerts.

Your travel agent will help you obtain a passport and tell you how you should care for it. He will know whether you need visas, special entry permits or particular immunizations.

He can also arrange for insurance, language study material, travelers' checks, mail, foreign currency exchange: in short, for all of the details that could wear you out before you begin your vacation.

But the travel agent's service isn't limited to taking care of physical aspects of your trip. He is also in a position to advise you on the quality of the accommodations at your destination. Having "scouted" the area

[5] Air Transport Association of America, "How to Fly" (Washington, D.C.: Air Transport Association of America pamphlet, 1969), p. 11.

himself, he can report first-hand on hotels and restaurants and the quality of their food and service.

2. Decide whether you want to fly first class or tourist class. If you have never flown, I would recommend that you seriously consider the advantages of going first class, particularly on longer flights and during busy travel seasons. As you gain further experience in flying, or if you fly off season, the distinction between first class and tourist class will become less important.

In first class, the seats are wider (reducing claustrophobic feelings), the meals are more elaborate, and you get more of a feeling of being pampered and taken care of. Also, you have more immediate access to the stewardesses should you feel the need for special attention.

3. An important decision these days (especially on overseas flights) is whether to take such standard planes as the Boeing 707, the DC-8 or the new "jumbo" Boeing 747. (In the near future, you will also have the choice of the McDonnell-Douglas DC-10 or the Lockheed TriStar L-1011 air bus.) Certainly the 747 gives one a feeling of great spaciousness and definitely reduces the feeling of claustrophobia which afflicts so many flyers. On the other hand, some flyers become overwhelmed by its sheer size and wonder how such a large plane can possibly stay aloft. All of these planes are, of course, equally safe. You should decide which one to take solely on the basis of your personal desires. Again, I want to point out that the more choice you can exercise, the more you gratify your own particular preferences, the more you take charge of your actions, the less anxiety you will feel.

4. Try to get sufficient rest before flying, especially on long flights. If you are well rested and physically comfortable, you will be better able to keep any tendencies toward anxiety in check. Experienced travelers recommend drinking lots of water and other fluids while aloft to counteract dehydration effects on long flights. (These are

due to the low humidity within the plane cabin.) Also recommended is loosening of ties, belts, and girdles, as well as wearing slippers instead of shoes.

Recent medical research indicates that "stress occurs when passengers fly east or west at high speed along the path of the earth's rotation, encountering hourly changes in the local time for each successive time zone that is crossed. The symptom complex which these rapid time changes can induce has been labeled 'circadian dysrhythmia.' " [6]

Aviation physicians recommend that "the jet-age passenger who wishes to avoid the difficulties associated with rapid time change should (1) depart well-rested, (2) choose daylight departures where possible, (3) exercise moderation in eating and drinking both before and during the flight and (4) plan no strenuous activities for the first twenty-four hours after arrival." [7]

The following medical information should prove reassuring to most flyers: [8]

> Age in itself is no reason to deny yourself the safety, speed, and comfort of travel by air. In fact, doctors say that the environment of today's pressurized and air-conditioned aircraft is ideal for the aged who have reasons to travel. "Older people with well-compensated cardiovascular and respiratory systems tolerate flight excellently," according to the American Medical Association and the Aerospace Medical Association.
>
> The same reassurance goes for those who have physical ailments and thus may hesitate to use any form of public transportation. As for airline travel, the American Medical Association says, "Travel by air has been found to be the most expeditious and desirable form of travel for patients with certain types of illnesses. Some

[6] George F. Catlett, "Circadian Dysrhythmia: A Jet Age Malady," *Modern Medicine,* August, 1970, p. 37.

[7] *Ibid.,* p. 124.

[8] "How to Fly," pp. 24–25.

patients may need a certain amount of preparation, but only a few will find that their condition makes it undesirable for them to travel by air."

Most people with heart ailments may fly without fear of aggravations, provided they are able to indulge in ordinary physical activity without undue fatigue, palpitation, shortness of breath, or chest pain. Air travel normally does not disturb those with high blood pressure. Asthmatics whose breathing problems are medically controlled will not as a rule be bothered in the air. In any case, always advise the airline of your physical handicap at the time your reservation is made so that any necessary special arrangements can be made.

Should you hesitate to fly if you are expecting a child? Medical authorities say that flying has no harmful effect upon a normal pregnancy. According to the air medical committee of the International Air Transport Association (IATA), "Expectant mothers may be accepted for carriage (by air) up to and including the 35th week of pregnancy." Some carriers will accept pregnant women within two weeks of confinement for short trips, provided a doctor's certificate is furnished stating that she has been examined and found physically fit for the trip. To be prepared for the unlikely event of a premature birth aloft, the major airlines give their cabin attendants appropriate instruction as part of their first-aid training course.

Others for whom flying creates no problem include persons with healed lesions resulting from tuberculosis, and diabetics. Surgical patients make excellent air passengers. However, they should be given adequate antibiotic therapy before flight, or arrangements should be made to administer antibiotics at stopovers during flight. In the past, the disabled person was often denied many of life's normal activities. Today, according to the American Rehabilitation Foundation, some 250,000 Americans in wheelchairs, more than 5,000,000 with heart conditions, 200,000 with heavy leg braces, and 140,000 with artificial limbs are adding a new dimension to life through travel.

What kind of care can a handicapped person expect from the airlines? Here's how a representative of a major U.S. airline summarized it: "When our agent makes a reservation for a handicapped person, he places him on the most lightly booked flight available so the cabin attendant will have more time to devote to him. He also notifies the passenger service staff at each airport the passenger will transit of the nature of the handicap and any special assistance the passenger may need. If any special diet is required, he notifies the commissaries along the line. If the patient has his own wheelchair and it is the lightweight, fold-up type that is easily portable, it may be carried free aboard the airplane."

A handicapped person need not worry about his reception at the end of his flight. Qualified personnel have been notified of his arrival and are prepared to offer all required assistance, including a wheelchair, if necessary. Should he be connecting with another flight, the airline involved has been notified. This is made possible through an agreement among the scheduled airlines that each carrier accepting a physically handicapped passenger who needs assistance must notify all other carriers that may be transporting the passenger on subsequent legs of his journey.

5. The choice of seats on a commercial airliner is very important to many passengers. Basically, the choices are whether to sit up front, in the middle, or in the rear of the plane. Also, whether to take an aisle seat, middle seat or a seat near the window. These choices have nothing to do with air safety. They are entirely matters of personal preference.

If you are an inexperienced flyer you would do well in most instances to choose an aisle seat. This will enable you to step into the aisle easily if you feel tense. Also, you do not have to look out of the window. Some people become extremely nervous while looking out the window of a plane, especially if they look straight down. This reminds them how high up they are and activates latent acrophobic tendencies.

Others prefer to sit next to the window because it is important for them to "see what is going on." If you do sit next to a window, you have the option of pulling down the shade; you need not look out unless you so desire.

Many fearful flyers become especially apprehensive when seated next to somebody who seems very calm and collected; it makes them feel foolish, childish, and "crazy" by comparison. Others derive comfort from sitting next to somebody who seems to have things under control. Still others become apprehensive if seated next to somebody who is manifestly nervous—as if they fear a contagion effect. Finally, some flyers like to sit next to a nervous flyer because it gives them a feeling of superiority. Again, exercise your own preferences. Do what makes you feel better.

Unfortunately, it is usually not possible to find out in advance whom you are going to sit next to, unless you travel with family or friends. Usually on overseas flights and on longer flights within the United States, you can select your seat prior to entering the plane. The earlier you check in, the more choices you will have. If you have particularly strong preferences in this matter, please do not hesitate to discuss them with the person who checks you in. Whenever possible, he will try to accommodate you.

6. The location of the restrooms is important to some flyers. Usually they want to be close to the restroom so that they can reach it quickly should they develop gastric or other unpleasant symptoms. Also, it serves as a kind of "escape hatch" for claustrophobic feelings. But remember, there is frequently a great deal of activity and traffic in the vicinity of the restrooms. If you are allergic to crowded conditions and to noise, the tensions engendered may outweigh the convenience of closeness.

Usually first-class sections have their own restrooms in the front of the plane. In tourist class, restrooms are usually located toward the rear of the plane. Galleys may be located in various parts of the planes, depending on the airline's specifications to the manufacturers. You can find out the exact location of restrooms and galleys at the time you check in for your flight.

7. Another question that bothers some fearful flyers is how early to come to the airport prior to departure. Obviously, if you come too late, you run the risk of missing the plane. On the other hand, if you arrive too early, you may generate too much anxiety while waiting. I would suggest you call the airport in advance to find out the earliest possible check-in time for your particular flight.

8. Some flyers have very definite preferences concerning which airports to use. In New York, for example, some prefer to depart or arrive from the largest airport, John F. Kennedy International. Others like smaller airports such as Newark and La Guardia. This again is strictly a matter of personal preference. It has nothing whatsoever to do with flight safety. If you become especially fearful in large crowds, you would do well to consider the possibility of departing from a smaller airport. On the other hand, if you believe that there is "safety in numbers," it would be better for you to depart from a larger airport. In this, as in all the choices we have been discussing, no two people are the same, and you should make your choices entirely on the basis of what pleases you most.

RELIEVING YOUR ANXIETY ON THE PLANE

A. Use of Alcohol

Alcohol can help you during a flight if your panic is not too great. You can obtain at least two drinks of liquor on most commercial flights. In addition, if you desire, you can order additional drinks at the airport prior to departure. Basically, what happens when you drink on a plane is that your thinking apparatus becomes somewhat dulled.

You tend to worry less about possible dangers. Drinking reduces the tendency toward "overideation" which afflicts so many fearful flyers. Thinking too much in a situation where little action is possible is not adaptive. It only makes you more anxious.

We should make a distinction between solitary and social drinking on a plane. If you drink on a plane in the company of people you like, you will usually feel better than if you drink alone. Some people find that alcohol makes them feel more cheerful; others feel sad when drinking. Take stock of how drinking affects you personally. If you find that it usually makes you feel better, by all means use it in moderation. If you find that it makes you more apprehensive, avoid it.

B. Tranquilizers, Sleeping Pills, Barbiturates

Many fearful flyers resort to the use of tranquilizers and sleeping pills during flight. These help in much the same way as alcohol does. They tend to diminish guilt feelings, reduce the level of anxiety, and make perceptions of reality less sharp. This dulling of perception need not disturb you since you do not have to make any important decisions on the plane. (Pilots and crew members who have to be fully alert throughout a flight are forbidden, by regulation, from drinking or using drugs at least twenty-four hours before flight time.)

Many people feel less anxious if they are not too sharply aware of their immediate environment. If this is true for you, taking drugs will help, provided you take them in proper dosage. Some people are phobic about taking any type of medication. If you are one of them, do not use them on the plane. You will only make yourself more anxious.

Drugs may be taken before or during a flight. But please, before using drugs, consult your personal physician. No two people react in exactly the same way. Your physician is the only one who can prescribe the drugs appropriate to your needs.

Some fearful flyers bring aboard kits containing various drugs, sleeping pills, alcohol, and other objects which they feel will help them in an emergency. They use a mechanism not too different from the child, fearful of the dark, who comforts himself by taking a favorite doll or toy to bed. As a psychologist, I am, of course, not in favor of dependency on magical techniques. However, I see no reason why you should not use any device which helps you on a flight, provided it is not harmful.

ACHIEVING MASTERY ABOARD THE PLANE

The main principle here is to reduce feelings of powerlessness on the plane by consciously initiating goal-directed behavior. Anybody who feels forcibly restrained, whether in reality or in fantasy, will develop anxiety. The inevitable restrictions on the passenger's mobility on a flight (e.g., having to be strapped into his seat) produce feelings of powerlessness. These, in turn, automatically engender anxiety and rage. (To demonstrate this phenomenon to yourself, lie on the floor with your arms held rigidly at your sides and your legs together. Ask several people to hold you so tightly that you are unable to move your muscles voluntarily. Notice how tense you become almost immediately.)

One of the most effective things you can do aboard a plane, once the "fasten seat belt" sign is off, is to *get up and move about.* Frightened passengers who sit rigidly in their seats throughout a flight are doing exactly the wrong thing! By immobilizing themselves in this way they only magnify their illusion of powerlessness and confirm their conviction that they have been robbed of all capacity for autonomous action. To counteract these feelings on a plane, think of all your actions (e.g., ordering a drink from the stewardesses, opening or closing a window shade, entering into a conversation with a nearby passenger) as evidence of your ability to exert some influence on the immediate situation.

In this connection, activities involving the use of your hands are usually better than more passive activities such as reading. Losing yourself in a movie aboard flight can be very helpful. Also useful are activities which require intense concentration, such as games, crossword puzzles, knitting, crocheting, and the like. Some passengers successfully avoid anxiety by busying themselves with paperwork. Others enjoy "logging the flight" (charting its course on maps, trying to guess exact arrival times, etc.).[9]

HELPFUL ATTITUDES DURING THE FLIGHT

If you are the type of person who is accustomed to having things under control at all times, the chances are you are hypersensitive to slight increases in the magnitude of your anxiety. Even a mild degree of anxiety may panic you because it goes contrary to your usual self-image.

I have personally accompanied many fearful flyers to airports and aboard planes. Often I am unable to detect any unusual overt anxiety in these flyers even though I know they are experiencing tremendous internal tensions. When I inform them that the anxiety which they regard as so catastrophic is not visible to a trained psychologist, they are usually quite surprised. If you are afraid of your own anxiety or having others see it, you are probably magnifying the problem out of all proportion. In most instances, your anxiety will be barely perceptible, if at all, to people around you. Although many fearful passengers

[9] One reason why pilots and stewardesses rarely develop anxiety on flights is that they are continuously engaged in goal-directed activities that require their full concentration.

are afraid of "making fools of themselves" on a plane, very, very few act in such a way as to call attention to themselves.

Another thought to keep in mind is that the take-off and landing phases of a flight which frighten so many flyers actually last only a few minutes. If you remind yourself that at most you will be nervous for no more than five or ten minutes, you will be less frightened. Conscious knowledge that anxiety will not continue indefinitely can be very helpful in preventing panic from setting in. Knowing when a "dangerous" situation will end reduces ambiguity and gives you partial control.

GETTING "FED UP" WITH YOUR FEAR OF FLYING

If you have been carefully following the psychological exercises and other steps described in this chapter, you are probably beginning to experience a certain degree of irritation with yourself for having let your fear of flying get you down. This feeling of irritation is, in my opinion, a hopeful sign. It indicates that your healthy ego is beginning to reassert itself.

Hopefully, at this point you will realize that you have been paying inordinate attention to your fears. Your symptoms, in a sense, have taken hold of you. You have hypnotized yourself into taking them seriously.

In this connection I would like to say that attempts to overcome fears of flying by "positive thinking" completely miss the point. If you try to outwit your phobia, if you try to muster all your forces to combat it, you endow it with more power than it deserves.

I think a more appropriate attitude would be: "I have had enough of this nonsense. My fears have drained too much of my energy and have prevented me from enjoying myself. I simply am not going to let them get me down. I will not even try to talk myself out of them. I will laugh at them and fly!"

I recall, in this connection, one fearful flyer who told me that he finally got to a point where he felt like kicking the nose of a plane in anger because he had allowed the plane to "vanquish" him. Shortly after expressing this thought, he was able to fly. He was able to override his fears by becoming angry at his fears instead of at himself.

This attitude, incidentally, can help you to deal with many interpersonal fears. A person can frighten or torment you only to the extent that you endow him with the power to do so. Once you can ignore him or, better still, laugh at him, he loses all power to upset you.

Eventually you will realize that by not flying or flying with fear you have been playing a big joke on yourself. You have allowed a series of nonsensical, absurd fantasies to gain the upper hand. You are the one who attributed undue power to these fears to begin with. You can reassert your rationality by becoming irritated with and finally laughing at these monsters of your own creation.

Unfortunately, you will not be able to become sufficiently fed up with your phobia *until* you have tried very hard to overcome it. There is no way of getting around the fact that this process takes time. However, *after* you have made all reasonable efforts to overcome your fears, switch gears. Don't maintain the fight indefinitely. Call a halt to it and fly.

HOW IMPULSE FLIGHTS CAN HELP

Start by taking an impulse flight to a nearby city. Impulse flying is particularly useful for people who develop anticipatory anxiety days, weeks, or even months before a flight. If this description fits you, I would recommend you take a number of short unplanned flights. Naturally, I do not recommend impulse flying if you are still overly anxious. It will only help if you have already begun to toy with the idea of taking a flight.

If you can bypass your anticipatory anxiety, you will usually find the actual flight to be much less frightening than you thought. The more often you are able to get aboard a plane, the less fear you will have. This is particularly true if you have never flown before or if you fly rarely.

So, if you feel an impulse to fly, do not squelch it! Drive to the airport and take a short flight. The destination is unimportant. What is important is to prove to yourself that you can actually fly.

Of course, it is even better if you fly together with friends who understand and accept your fear of flying. I have seen many instances in which two or more fearful flyers helped themselves enormously by banding together and flying on the spur of the moment. Flying with other fearful flyers whom you like is one of the most effective ways of allaying fears. It eliminates feelings of isolation and provides invaluable group support. The potent role of group support in overcoming fears of flying will be discussed in Chapter 8.

CHAPTER 7

Short-Term Professional Techniques to Overcome Fears of Flying

IF, AFTER FOLLOWING THE STEPS outlined in the previous chapter, you still cannot fly, you should consider the possibility of obtaining short-term professional help. You may need the services of a professional psychotherapist to (1) help you gain further insight, (2) give you additional support and (3) offer additional leads on how best to deal with your fears.

Many people are not aware that it is possible to get professional help for pinpointed problems such as the flying phobia without having to undergo extensive psychotherapy. Nor do they realize that psychoanalytic methods have been supplemented, in recent years, by behavioral modification techniques, which greatly increase the therapist's efficacy in working with phobias.[1] Marked improvement in less than fifteen sessions is not uncommon.

[1] The following sources deal with therapeutic handling of phobic reactions: Burton A. Glick, "Conditioning Therapy in Phobias," *American Journal of Psychotherapy*, XXIV (1970), 99–101; Arnold A. Lazarus, "Group Therapy of Phobic Disorders by Systematic Deconditioning," *Journal of Abnormal and Social Psychology*, LXIII (1961); Evelyn P. Ivey, "Recent Advances in the Psychiatric Diagnosis and Treatment of Phobias," *American Journal of Psychotherapy*, XII (1963), 35–50; G. Donald MacClean and Robert W. Graff, "Behavioral Bibliotherapy: A Simple Home Remedy for Fears," *Psychotherapy*, VII (1970), 118–119; Louis Paul, "The Suicidal Self," *Psychotherapy*, VII (1970), 177–180; Frederick A. Perls, *Gestalt Theory Verbatim* (Lafayette, Calif.: Real People Press, 1969); Lewis R. Wolberg, *The Tech-*

If you recognize that your fear of flying is caused by emotional factors and if you are seriously motivated to do something about it, short-term psychotherapy can be enormously helpful. I stress motivation here because I believe it to be absolutely essential if you are to get maximal benefits from short-term therapy. If you are not strongly motivated and engage in protracted struggles with the therapist, you will only sabotage your efforts to fly.

The first step is to locate a qualified therapist. You may already know of a therapist of high repute in your area. If not, departments of psychology or psychiatry at nearby universities will supply you with the names of competent psychologists and psychiatrists.

The Appendix to this book contains a list of leading associations of psychiatrists, psychologists, and hypnotherapists in the United States. By writing to their central offices you will be able to obtain the names of qualified therapists in your own area. Many of these associations also publish directories of their members. You can consult these at your local library.

SHORT-TERM PSYCHOANALYTIC APPROACHES

I would like to describe how a professional therapist might typically work with your fears of flying in short-term, psychoanalytically oriented psychotherapy.[2] My assumption is that if you know what to expect *prior* to going to a therapist, you will get more rapid and effective results.

---

nique of Psychotherapy (New York: Grune & Stratton, 1967), Vol. II; Joseph Wolpe, *The Practice of Behavior Therapy* (New York: Elmsford, 1969); and Manuel D. Zane, "How One Psychiatrist Utilizes His Tape Recorder with Patients," *Frontiers of Clinical Psychiatry,* December, 1969.

[2] Based in part on Wolberg, pp. 923–930.

1. First, he would attempt to set you at ease so as to enable you to discuss your fears of flying, as well as other fears, with a minimum of embarrassment. The more open and frank you can be, the more quickly he will be able to help you.

2. He would then ask you to describe your conscious fears of flying. You can save time by bringing a precise list of your fears to the first session. The more detailed this list, the better. If at all possible, rank your fears from the most frightening to the least.

3. At the beginning of Chapter 6 I outlined certain ways to gain access to the unconscious wishes and fears you have attached to flying. These include the use of word associations, drawings, daydreams, and dreams. It would help the therapist and save time for both of you if you brought him this material in the first session.

4. After your initial presentation the therapist would ask you additional questions. (Therapists who utilize short-term techniques are much more active than those who do "regular" psychotherapy. They "zero in" as quickly as possible.) He might ask you to describe briefly what was going on in your life situation just prior to the development of your fear of flying. If you have never flown, he might ask you at what age you first became apprehensive about flying. If you have flown and suddenly found yourself unable to do so, he might want to know what was going on at the time in other areas of your life.

5. He might then ask you if you have any hunches regarding the causes of your fear of flying. Also, whether you can connect these fears to other disturbing events that took place either before or after the development of your fear of flying.

6. He might want to know what you have done to help yourself in the past and why you think these previous attemps were not successful.

7. He would be interested in finding out whether you have or have had (however fleetingly) other phobias such

as claustrophobia, acrophobia, or any of the other phobias mentioned in Chapter 4. Again, he would want to know when they started and whether you can connect them with specific precipitating events.

8. He would, in all likelihood, take a brief history of your formative years, particularly with regard to childhood phobias.

9. By this time the therapist will have developed certain hypotheses concerning the underlying causes of your fears. He will have determined whether the phobia is triggered by guilt over unacceptable impulses, whether it is primarily related to separation anxiety, or both. He will also have formed some conclusion as to whether or not it is complicated by marital or family problems.

10. In rare instances he may resort to hypnoanalysis in order to help you recover deeply repressed memories which may be crucial to an understanding of your phobia.

11. As soon as the therapist feels confident that he understands the symbolic meaning of your phobia, and as soon as he feels that you are ready to understand his interpretations, he will explain things to you in clear, simple language. He will help you to become aware of exactly what impulses or fears are being stirred up. He will also give you some clues as to which specific stimuli in the phobic situation are triggering your anxiety. Finally, he will advise you on how best to handle your phobia based on his estimate of the strength and nature of your defenses vis-à-vis the amount of anxiety you evidence.

Let me give you a specific example of how he might help you handle your fears.

Recently, in working with a female patient who had a severe phobic reaction to flying, I realized that she was unconsciously using her phobia to control her husband. Each time he indicated that he was eager to fly, she frustrated him by developing anxiety attacks of such severity that they were unable to fly. I recommended to her that the next time she experienced phobic symptoms prior to a flight she repeat consciously to herself that she was using her symptoms to prevent her husband (and herself) from flying. Once she grasped the idea that her "fear of flying" had nothing to do with flight but was rather a manifestation of a power struggle with her husband, she was able to fly. Some anxiety remained temporarily but it was controllable. Later, she was motivated to explore why she chose fear of flying as her main battleground and why she could not assert herself more directly with her husband.

If your flying phobia is of recent origin, if it is not associated with other phobias, if you do not derive secondary benefits from it (as in the case just cited), and if the intensity of your anxiety is not overwhelming, it is very possible that you will be able to get considerable relief from short-term, psychoanalytically oriented therapy within one to eight sessions.

In many instances the insight you obtain by psychoanalytic methods will be sufficient to "desymbolize" the phobia; you will no longer attach basic anxieties to flight. In some cases, however, such insight will not be enough. The therapist will then supplement the psychoanalytic approach with other techniques.

HYPNOTIC APPROACHES

Hypnosis may be very useful in overcoming fears of flying provided it is administered by a qualified psychologist or psychiatrist. Preferably, he should be a member of the American Society of Clinical Hypnosis or the Society for Clinical and Experimental Hypnosis. (See the Appendix for a list of associations of qualified professionals.)

Following is a sample of one technique utilized by Dr. Lewis R. Wolberg, a leading psychiatrist and hypnotherapist. Please remember that it is presented for purposes of illustration only—to give you a feel of what hypnosis is like. If you consult a professional for your fear of flying, he will tailor his approach to your specific needs. Each person and each problem requires a different approach. *Only* a qualified professional can determine the method best suited to you.

Now just settle back and shut your eyes. Breathe in deeply through your nostrils or mouth, right down into the pit of your stomach. D-e-e-p-l-y, d-e-e-p-l-y, d-e-e-p-l-y; but not so deeply that you are uncomfortable. Just deeply enough so that you feel the air soaking in. In . . . and out. D-e-e-p-l-y, d-e-e-p-l-y. In . . . and out. And as you feel the air soaking in, you begin to feel yourself getting t-i-r-e-d and r-e-l-a-x-e-d. Very r-e-l-a-x-e-d. Even d-r-o-w-s-y, d-r-o-w-s-y, and relaxed.

Now I want you to concentrate on the muscle groups that I point out to you. Loosen them, relax them while visualizing them. You will notice that you may be tense in certain areas and the idea is to relax yourself completely. Concentrate on your forehead. Loosen the muscles around your eyes. Your eyelids relax. Now your face, your face relaxes. And your mouth . . . relax the muscles around your mouth and even the inside of your mouth. Your chin; let it sag and feel heavy. And as you relax your muscles, your breathing continues r-e-g-u-l-a-r-l-y and d-e-e-p-l-y, deeply within yourself. Now your neck relaxes. Every muscle, every fiber in your neck relaxes. Your shoulders . . . relax . . . your arms . . . your elbows . . . your forearms . . . your wrists . . . your hands . . . and your fingers relax. Your arms feel loose and limp, heavy and loose and limp. Your whole body begins to feel loose and limp. Your neck muscles relax; the front of your neck, the back muscles. If you wish, wiggle your head if necessary to get all the kinks out. Keep breathing deeply and relax. Now your chest. The front part of your chest relaxes . . . and the back part of your chest relaxes. Your abdomen . . . the pit of your stomach, that relaxes. The small of your back, loosen the muscles. Your hips . . . your thighs . . . your knees relax . . . even the muscles in your legs. Your ankles . . . your feet . . . and your toes. Your whole body feels loose and limp. [Pause.] And now, as you feel the muscles relaxing, you will notice that you begin to feel relaxed and tired all over. Your body begins to feel v-e-r-y, v-e-r-y tired . . . and you are going to feel d-r-o-w-s-i-e-r and d-r-o-w-s-i-e-r, from the top of your head right down to your toes. Every breath you take is going to soak in deeper and deeper and deeper, and you feel your body getting drowsier and drowsier.

And now I want you to imagine, to visualize the most relaxed and quiet and pleasant scene imaginable. Visualize a relaxed and pleasant quiet scene. Any scene that is comfortable. It can be some scene in your past, or a scene you project in the future. It can be nothing more than being at the beach watching the water breaking on the shore. Or a lake with a sailboat floating lazily by. Or merely looking at the blue sky with one or two billowy clouds moving slowly. Any scene that is quiet and pleasant and makes you feel drowsy. Or a sound like Beethoven's sonata, or any other selection that is soothing! Drowsier and drowsier and drowsier. You are v-e-r-y weary, and every breath will send you in deeper and deeper and deeper.

As you visualize this quiet scene I shall count from one to twenty, and when I reach the count of twenty, you will feel yourself in deep. [The count should be made very slowly.] One, deeper, deeper, two, deeper and deeper and deeper. Three . . . drowsier and drowsier. Four, deeper and deeper. Five . . . drowsier and drowsier and drowsier. Six . . . seven, very tired, very relaxed. Eight, deeper and deeper. Nine . . . ten, drowsier and drowsier. Eleven, twelve, thirteen, deeper and deeper. D-r-o-w-s-i-e-r and d-r-o-w-s-i-e-r. Fourteen, drowsier and drowsier and drowsier. Fifteen . . . sixteen . . . seventeen, deeper and deeper. Eighteen . . . nineteen . . . and finally twenty.

Now relax and rest for a minute or so, going deeper, d-e-e-p-e-r, d-e-e-p-e-r, and in a minute or so I shall talk to you and you will be more deeply relaxed. [Pause for one minute.]

In summary there are four things we are going to accomplish as a result of these exercises, the 4 S's: symptom relief, self-confidence, situation control and self-understanding. First, your various symptoms [enumerate] are going to be less and less upsetting to you. You will pay less and less attention to them, because they will bother you less and less. You will find that you have a desire to overcome them more and more. As we work at your problem, you will feel that your self-confidence grows and expands. You will feel more assertive and stronger. You will be able to handle yourself better in any situations that come along, particularly those that tend to upset you [enumerate]. Finally, and most importantly, your understanding of yourself will improve. You will understand better and better what is behind your trouble, how it started and why your symptoms developed. Whenever you feel your symptoms coming on, you will be able to understand what is bringing them about, and you will be able to do something constructive about this, more and more easily. You will continue working on what is behind your problem. [Pause.]

Relax and rest and, if you wish, give yourself all the necessary suggestions to *yourself* to feel better. Use the word "you." Take as long as you want. Then you can go to sleep or arouse yourself. When you are ready, you will arouse *yourself* no matter when that is, by counting slowly to yourself from one to five. You will be completely out of it then—aware and alert. Remember, the more you practice, the more intense will be your response, the more easily will your resistances give way. Keep on practicing. And now go ahead— relax—and when you are ready—wake *yourself* up.[3]

BEHAVIORAL MODIFICATION TECHNIQUES

You probably have heard of a common condition in children called "school phobia." Some children suddenly

[3] This example of hypnosis appears *ibid.,* pp. 893–896. Reprinted by permission of Dr. Wolberg and Grune & Stratton, Inc.

develop acute panic at the prospect of going to school; they simply cannot bring themselves to attend. This is not a matter of truancy or laziness. It is an actual dread of going to school. Usually (although not always) the longer the child stays away from school, the more difficult it is for him to return. Many therapists who work with school phobias insist that the child be returned to school as soon as possible even if he does not initially attend classes. Once inside the school, the child frequently loses much of his anxiety. Gradually, with additional support and insight, he is able to attend classes on his own.

In working with phobic adults the therapist cannot physically confront the patient with the frightening situation, but the principle is the same as in working with school phobias. Sooner or later the therapist must get the patient to approach the phobic situation—initially in fantasy, later in reality.

Behavioral modification techniques have proven extremely useful in the treatment of phobias.[4] These techniques derive from modern learning theory. They are highly effective in desensitizing phobic reactions, particularly if the phobias are relatively uncomplicated and circumscribed. They may be used independently or in conjunction with psychoanalytic techniques.

The behavioral therapist is generally less inclined than the psychoanalytically oriented clinician to view phobias as symptomatic of unconscious conflicts. Rather, he focuses directly on the manifest behavior and attempts to change it without exploring its unconscious antecedents. Some therapists,[5] however, *combine* psychoanalytic and behavioral modification techniques. Thus, in working with a particular phobia, they may start with psychoanalytic

[4] See especially Wolpe.
[5] See Glick. This article discusses how psychoanalytic and behavioral modification techniques may be combined in working with phobias.

techniques and later supplement these with behavioral approaches; in other instances, the sequence is reversed.

Dr. Edward Dengrove uses the following material to introduce patients to systematic desensitization, a commonly used behavioral modification technique. I would like to quote it to give you an idea of how such techniques are typically applied in practice:

The type of treatment that is being offered to you is known as systematic desensitization. It is based upon scientific studies of conditioned reflexes and is particularly helpful to persons who are fearful. It makes little difference what these fears are: whether of closed places, or being alone, walking alone, driving or flying; or whether one fears loss of self-control, criticism by others, and the like.

Kindly list *all* of the fears that disturb you. Make the list as complete as possible. We will go over the list together and reduce it to its basic units. Treatment will be directed to each individual fear.

The next step will be to teach you how to relax. There are several methods by which this may be accomplished. The particular method that suits your needs will be chosen. This is very important, for the more relaxed you are, the more rapid your progress to health. You cannot be relaxed and remain anxious or fearful at the same time.

When you are completely relaxed—not partially, but completely—I shall present to your visual imagination a series of situations. These will be based upon your present fears. They will be organized in series, graded from the most mild to the most intense. Each forms a hierarchy.

As you visualize each scene in the relaxed state, you may find yourself unmoved by what you see. Or you may experience an uneasiness or restlessness (anxiety). This is a critical point in treatment, and must be signalled to me. No matter how slight, I must be made aware of it.

I may ask, "Do you feel relaxed? Do you feel at ease?" If you do, then move your head up and down ever so slightly. If you do not, move it from side to side.

This is a critical point, for we can only proceed as fast as you are able to accept these visualized situations with ease. I shall not push or prod you. It is only by the ability to maintain your relaxed state that you are able to overcome these fears.

The desensitization takes place gradually by getting you to cope with small doses of anxiety at first, then gradually increasing the dosages a small amount at a time.

With children, desensitization is done in a less subtle manner. Consider a child who is afraid of dogs. The child is held by a trusted person who allows him to suck on a lollipop and point to a dog on a leash in the distance. A little later, the child, still held, is encouraged to view a dog through a pet show window. Still later, he is brought closer to a dog; and later, closer still. With the pleasure of the food and security of being held by a trusted person, the child gradually overcomes his fear. At first there are pictures of dogs, then toy dogs, small, friendly dogs, medium-sized dogs, and so forth. At last, he will be able to reach out and touch a dog.

This gives you a clue to a second part of treatment. You are to do the very things that you fear. One cannot overcome a fear by avoiding it, as you have done in the past, nor by trying to drown it out with continued medication. Medicine is helpful, but only a crutch, to be reduced and gradually thrown away.

The same principles of gradual desensitization must be employed. You are not to attempt any activity that produces overwhelming anxiety. However, you can and should try those tasks that are only mildly upsetting, at the same time attempting to quiet yourself. If the anxiety persists, stop what you are doing, for this will only set you back. Instead, return to doing those things that you can do without getting upset.

With this approach you will find yourself gradually

doing more of these tasks that you avoided in the past. One can get used to almost any new situation that is approached gradually.

Interestingly, as the milder fears are overcome, the more strong ones lose their intensity and lessen, much as the contents of a gum machine diminish with the discharge of each piece of gum. The more one attempts with relaxation, the more rapid the improvement. But one must keep in mind that these attempts deal only with those productive of mild anxiety.

A warning: everyone must proceed at his or her own pace. Some slowly, others more rapidly. There is no reason to feel guilt or shame if one's progress is slow. The process of desensitization cannot be hurried by rushing into highly anxious situations. You will not be thrown into the water and made to swim or sink on your own. At times, under the pressure of need or anger, a few of you will make large strides but this is the exception to the rule.

Consider the woman who is afraid to leave her home. Her first move is to step outside her front door and back again to the house. From there she gradually makes it to the street in front of her home, then around the house—by herself or with someone or while someone trusted is in the house. Each day this is extended until she is able to walk a house away, then two houses, then half a block; with someone, without someone, with someone at home, with no one there. Again, no new step is made until the previous step is mastered, and until it can be accomplished without any anxiety whatsoever. Each fear is attacked individually, daily or as frequently as this can be done.

Gradually, you find yourself doing things without thinking about them. Sometimes it will be only after you have done something that you realize you have done it without forethought of anxiety. It may be that someone else will point out to you that you have done something you would not have attempted in the past.

A cooperative spouse is not only helpful and understanding but an essential part of this approach. He or she can be tremendously important to this undertaking. Marital problems tend to hold back progress and should be resolved.

It is by doing what we do in the office, and what you do for yourself away from the office, that will lead you to health. One or other of these techniques may be used alone, but when both are employed, progress is so much faster. Amaze yourself.[6]

The principles involved in systematic desensitization are: [7]

1. The state of relaxation induced is rewarding (pleasurable) in itself; therefore, it tends to counterbalance anxiety, at least partially.

2. The person's confidence in the therapist and his belief in his desire to help him gives him courage to proceed closer to the painful stimuli.

3. By repeatedly facing the "dangerous" stimuli without punishment the subject obtains a form of gratification. Eventually this gratification outweighs the pain and discomfort originally associated with the stimuli.

If, after the application of the above type of conditioning techniques, you still hesitate to fly, the therapist will encourage you to take matters more into your own hands. He will ask you to bring yourself as close as possible physically to the phobic situation. He might, for example, ask you to take a taxi or drive yourself to the airport. At the next session, he might ask you to report to him exactly what you actually felt, at what point the anxiety began to manifest itself, and what you did about it. In succeeding sessions he would ask you to get closer to the plane, perhaps even to sit in it briefly and see what feelings you experience there. He would offer you encouragement after

[6] Edward Dengrove, quoted in Wolberg, pp. 820–822. Reprinted by permission of Dr. Wolberg and Grune & Stratton, Inc.
[7] For a more detailed discussion of the theory of systematic desensitization, see Wolpe.

each success. At still a later session he might ask you to take a short flight. When you return, he would ask you to tell him exactly when you began to feel anxiety and what you did about it. The more skill you develop in noticing what stimuli trigger the phobic reaction and exactly what you do to handle it the more you will be able to bring the entire phobic sequence under conscious control.

I have found it extremely helpful, in difficult cases, to accompany patients to airports. There are two advantages to this: (1) The patient, literally, has somebody with him on whom he can depend. (2) It affords me an opportunity to see exactly what triggers his anxiety and how he handles it. I do not have to rely solely on his verbal account of what transpires.

In most instances your therapist will not be able to accompany you to the airport himself, because of time limitations. I would recommend, therefore, that you ask your spouse or some trusted friend to go with you to the airport or, preferably, on a flight itself. At your next session this person could report to the therapist exactly what he noticed in your behavior. This procedure not only aids the therapist; it provides you with additional support.

If you overcome your flying phobia by means of short-term psychotherapy, you might feel quite satisfied with the results and the matter will end there. If you decide to look further into other areas of anxiety and conflict, you have the option of continuing with the same therapist or, possibly, with a different therapist at a later date.

In closing, I want to reassure you that:

1. It is possible to treat a flying phobia effectively without undergoing extensive psychotherapy.

2. Getting rid of your flying phobia does not mean that you will develop other substitutive symptoms. On the contrary, being able to fly without anxiety will in all likelihood increase your confidence in other areas of functioning.

CHAPTER 8

How to Overcome
Your Fear of Flying
by Group Techniques

GROUP TECHNIQUES ARE extremely effective in overcoming phobic fears of flying. If the self-help methods described in Chapter 6 and the short-term, therapeutic approaches described in Chapter 7 have not sufficiently reduced your phobia, I would strongly recommend that you consider joining such a group.

In this chapter I shall tell you how to organize these groups and discuss some of the basic principles leading to their successful operation. The first step is to get together a congenial group of friends or acquaintances who are afraid to fly. Taking such a step requires considerable initiative, but initiative is essential in any attempt to overcome phobic reactions. Ideally, the size of the group should vary between ten and twenty persons. It might be possible to work with as few as four or five or as many as twenty-five, but ten to twenty is the optimal size.

If you cannot get a large enough group from your immediate circle, announce to the membership of your clubs or associations that a group specifically set up to combat flying fears is to be formed. Also, you might consider the possibility of announcing the formation of a flying group in your local newspaper. Be careful, however, because such advertisements sometimes attract people who are looking for personal therapy, "encounters," "growth experiences" and the like. If you specify that the goal of these groups is solely to overcome flying fears, most of the applicants will probably be serious, well-motivated individuals whose primary purpose is to fly as quickly as possible.

Consider seriously the possibility of approaching major airlines in your area to request their aid. They will usually cooperate with individuals and especially with groups of people who wish to overcome fears of flying. Unfortunately, they do not officially sponsor groups to help fearful flyers at this time. (I hope they do in the future, because they are in the best position to provide the professional and educational facilities necessary for the most effective functioning of such groups.)

The next step is to obtain the services of a trained psychologist, psychiatrist or psychiatric social worker who specializes in group therapy. It is *absolutely essential* that these groups be led by a competent professional. A list of names and addresses of such professionals in your area can be obtained by writing to the American Group Psychotherapy Association (see Appendix) or by consulting its directory in your local library. (A psychologist or psychiatrist is not permitted to advertise his services to the public.)

If no members of the AGPA practice in your area, obtain the names and addresses of qualified psychologists, psychiatrists and psychiatric social workers who are members of the other organizations listed in the Appendix. (Some of these are trained in group techniques but, for a variety of reasons, have not yet joined AGPA.)

In all forms of psychotherapy, the therapist's training and experience are the most important factors in ensuring positive results. Ordinarily, his superficial personality characteristics are of lesser importance. However, in developing a group flying program the overt personality of the therapist is a prime consideration. It is essential that he manifest leadership qualities and that he inspire confidence. As I mentioned in Chapter 1, fearful flyers, particularly in the early phases of the program, tend to form a strong dependency on the leader. They need reassurance that he is "strong," that he will not fail them, and that he will be available in times of panic. (On more than one occasion, fearful flyers have called me from an airport immediately prior to taking a flight. Just hearing my voice provided enough reassurance to enable them to fly.)

In psychoanalytic group therapy, therapists normally discourage such strong dependency on the leader. In groups of fearful flyers, by contrast, it is essential that group members look up to the leader.

Following is an outline of the typical course of a group program for people who are afraid to fly.

1. The leader personally interviews each applicant. Most applicants will probably be reasonably stable. However, in some instances the leader may determine that participation in a group would be too upsetting to a particular individual. Only a trained therapist can make this type of decision!

Any applicant who is very argumentative or continuously challenges the value of the experience should *not* be encouraged to start, since the success of the program requires that positive feelings and rapport exist among all group members.

The group should be strictly limited to fearful flyers. The presence of non-fearful flyers arouses tremendous resentment in these groups.

2. After the group leader has screened applicants, he outlines the group program. The more structure he can provide at the outset, the more valuable the experience will be for all concerned.

Normally he stipulates that the group will meet once weekly for one and a half hours. He may additionally recommend that members convene without him for approximately one half hour prior to the regular session and one half hour afterward. (This added time together promotes group cohesion.)

3. The physical setting is important. The group should meet in a living or conference room with a comfortable clublike atmosphere. It is desirable, although not essential, that photographs of various types of aircraft and travel posters be hung on the walls.

4. The leader announces that the first five group sessions will be devoted primarily to a discussion of fears of flying. These sessions are to be followed by one or two educational sessions at which invited safety experts, pilots and other airline personnel answer factual questions raised by members of the group. This will be followed by an additional seven or eight meetings devoted primarily to further elaboration of the fears of group members and recommendations by the leader on how to overcome these fears.

5. He delineates certain rules for the functioning of the group:

A. Each member will have an opportunity to talk about his phobic fears in as much detail as possible. (Most group members will be extremely grateful for this, having received little sympathy from non-fearful flyers in the past.)

B. Each group member will be asked to bring in the two drawings described in Chapter 5. He will also be invited to present any dreams he has ever had about flying. As each group member tells his dream, the others try to identify with it and relate it to something in themselves. The leader does not request the dreamer to give personal associations to his dream. (However, these are not discouraged, if spontaneously offered.) The other group members are requested to refrain from "interpreting" the dreamer's personality. The dream is fundamentally a "group property," not a vehicle for explorations of the dreamer's personality.

C. The group leader introduces at propitious times the psychological exercises described in Chapter 5. If any of the exercises precipitate a temporary burst of anxiety in any of the group members he asks them to indicate this to him and takes necessary steps to keep the anxiety from getting out of hand.

D. Group members are requested *not* to verbalize any negative feelings they have toward one another. They may express negative feelings toward the group leader if they so desire, but not to one another. The rationale for this prohibition is that it is essential that strong positive feeling develop among the group members. Expressions of hostility not only do not help but are detrimental to the achievement of the group task.

The entire focus here is on *working cooperatively;* the task of each group member is to get himself to fly and, if possible, to help others to fly.

E. If group members wish to discuss personal matters with the group leader (especially if they develop anxiety about material brought up in the group), they may do so either before or after a session. Or they might write these down and hand them to the leader. Intensely personal matters, other than those dealing with fears of flying, should not be discussed in the group.

Those of you who have been in analytic group therapy or have read about it or have spoken to friends or acquaintances who have experienced it will recognize how different these flying groups are from psychoanalytically oriented groups. In the latter groups, no holds are barred. Each member is encouraged to talk about his thoughts and feelings with as little censorship as possible. The therapist attempts to elicit as many feelings, both positive and negative, toward other group members and toward himself as possible.

In psychoanalytically oriented therapy groups, the therapist's primary goal is to work through core personality problems of each member of the group. In the flying group, his goal is to help everybody to fly.

Technically, I would classify flying groups as "homogeneous, task-oriented, short-term groups." For those of you who wish to read further about psychoanalytic groups, I would suggest the following books and articles listed in the Selected References at the conclusion of the book: Marvin L. Aronson, "Patient Selection in Group Therapy," "Resistance in Individual and Group Psychotherapy," "Organization of Programs of Conjoint Psychotherapy in Mental Hygiene Clinics," "Technical Problems in Combined Therapy," and "Acting Out in Individual and Group Psychotherapy"; Sam Blum, "Group Therapy: A Special Report"; Ted Burke, "The Group Movement in America"; Asya L. Kadis, Jack D. Krasner, Charles Winick, and S. H. Foulkes, *A Practicum of Group Psychotherapy;* Alexander Wolf, "Short-Term Group Psychotherapy"; and Alexander Wolf and Emanuel K. Schwartz, *Psychoanalysis in Groups.*

In the first five sessions of the group, the leader utilizes many of the techniques described in Chapters 6 and 7. In addition to encouraging the group members to talk about their fears, he works with their associations, drawings, daydreams, and dreams specifically related to the theme of flying. The chief advantage of using these techniques in a group setting is that each group member is able to identify with others who share his fears and gains enormous support from the entire group—much more support than he could ordinarily get from an individual therapist.

You may be wondering how the group leader can work with so many people simultaneously. A trained group therapist is able to spot, after two or three sessions, certain phobic clusters among the group members. On the basis of his clinical experience he can usually determine whether a particular phobia derives principally from guilt feelings over sexual and assertive impulses, or separation anxiety, or some combination of these; also whether or not the phobia is complicated by marital or family difficulties. He is also able to determine which members need special support or other tailor-made approaches. He does not ordinarily verbalize his opinions about these matters in the group, but they influence his judgment on when and how to intervene.

During the first five sessions the therapist's chief tasks are to build cohesion in the group and to understand the unconscious determinants of the flying fears expressed. He indicates to the group members that insight, while very helpful, is not *crucial* to their flying successfully. He points out that many individuals who participate in this type of group are able to fly with only minimal insight. The purpose of this is to avoid discouraging group members who have only limited insight at this point.

During this first phase of the group program the organizers of the group should contact local representatives of the major airlines. They should request the airlines to send personnel who can answer technical questions about flying and who are familiar with safety procedures. Travel agents can also provide useful information to non-flyers in the group on how to arrange trips efficiently and pleasurably. Needless to say, the group's organizers should not enter into any financial arrangements with either airlines or travel agencies.

After the fifth group session one, or possibly two, educational meetings are set aside to deal with realistic aspects of flight and travel. In these sessions group members are encouraged to ask any questions that they wish about flying. The flying experts answer these questions frankly and in as much detail as necessary. The group leader need not be present at these meetings, but even if he is, the focus should be on the acquisition of information about flying.

In my experience group members benefit greatly from personal contacts with airline representatives. Not only do they learn valuable information which allays their unrealistic fears, but also they feel much reassured by personal contact with these highly competent professionals. Many people still do not sufficiently differentiate between the "daredevil" pilot of the past and the competent, highly trained men who make commercial aviation their career.

Flying experts are not brought in until the group has met for five full sessions. If they enter earlier, some group members (particularly the men) may become unduly obsessed with "facts and figures." After five sessions most members realize fully that they are dealing with a psychological problem and the acquisition of additional technical knowledge does not ordinarily deflect them from focusing on emotional aspects of their flying problem.

Some members with milder forms of flying fears may be able to fly by themselves after only five group sessions and one or two educational sessions. Some will fly even sooner.

Many members, however, will require seven or eight additional meetings.

In the second phase of the program some exploration of dreams, fantasies, word associations, and drawings continues, but the chief focus is on getting the members to fly. During this phase the group leader has four essential functions:

1. To ascertain which devices each group member characteristically uses to deal with his anxiety.

2. To reinforce these techniques and suggest additional ones on the basis of his understanding of the flyer's personality.

3. To introduce group-behavior modification and deconditioning methods.[1]

4. To accentuate group morale and cohesion wherever possible.

Early in the second phase of the program the group organizers should arrange for the entire group to visit an airport together and, if at all possible, to meet in a stationary airliner for approximately one hour. (Hopefully, the airlines will someday provide facilities whereby fearful

[1] For a discussion of certain behavioral modification techniques in a group setting, see Arnold A. Lazarus, "Group Therapy of Phobic Disorders by Systematic Deconditioning," *Journal of Abnormal and Social Psychology,* LXIII (1961).

flyers could experience simulated flights. This would prove enormously helpful in achieving rapid deconditioning of many simple fears.) It is essential that the leader accompany the group to the airport and to the stationary plane, if available. He encourages group members to talk about their fears at every step of the way and offers them practical advice on how to handle their fears as effectively as possible.

After this trip to the airport, if not earlier, a tremendous cohesion will have developed among group members. Having shared a common problem for approximately two months, they will inevitably become quite attached to one another and to the leader; many personal friendships will have developed.[2]

Morale in the group is usually so high at this point that some members spontaneously express a desire to take a group flight. Of course, the idea that traveling with friends will stave off disaster is irrational. If a plane is going to crash, it makes no difference whether or not one knows anyone else on the plane. Nevertheless, the feeling that one can share what he considers a dangerous experience with friends is tremendously supportive. There is no reason not to capitalize on this in overcoming the fear of flying.

After about the tenth group session the group leader announces a target date at which time all group members will take a short flight together to some nearby city. If there is an upsurgence of anxiety at this point, the leader may temporarily postpone the trip, but it is very important that as soon as the initial anxiety is worked through, a final target date be set and kept to. In the earlier phases of the program the phobic flyer's tendency to avoid the dangerous situation should be respected, but at this stage group pressures to fly can be very beneficial.

---

[2] This intense feeling of "groupness" results not only from having shared the same experiences but also from the homogeneity of socioeconomic background discussed in Chapter 1.

Not infrequently, some of the more adventurous group members encourage or even "dare" the more fearful flyers to fly. If any group member has flown individually during the course of the program he is encouraged to describe his experiences in the group. This provides a tremendous inspiration to the fearful members who have never flown. This is a special advantage of working with flying phobias in a group setting.

The group leader becomes increasingly active at this point to maintain the group's momentum. His emphasis is exclusively on getting the group members to fly. The leader reiterates that it is possible to fly successfully as a group, even though some members still have only a dim awareness of the underlying causes of their fears. (This is made possible through their identification with other group members.) Such a statement is necessary to avoid feelings of discouragement on the part of those group members who have not yet achieved some insight.

The next step is to fly! Again, if the group organizers contact the airlines I think they will find them extremely helpful and cooperative. In many cases they will facilitate travel arrangements to make the flight as pleasant as possible. They may, for example, recommend the best times to depart (to avoid stacking delays), offer suggestions as to the most convenient destination, etc.

It is absolutely essential that the leader personally accompany the group members on this flight. His physical presence may be indispensable to the success of the flight. During the flight he makes himself available to all group members. He listens to any personal comments they choose to make about their fears, offers on-the-spot advice and guidance, and meets with them, if at all possible, at the destination airport.

After the flight has been successfully completed the group members and the leader reconvene and discuss all of their reactions to the flight. Following a successful flight many group members will feel no need to proceed further.

They will be quite satisfied with having achieved their aim of flying.

The leader indicates that further sessions might help consolidate their gains, but he makes no attempt to keep reluctant members in the program. He might suggest that the group meet for periodic reunions, or possibly take additional group flights together, but these alternatives should be completely optional. It is inadvisable to make successful flyers overly dependent on the group. They are encouraged to fly on their own as soon as possible.

Some group members may want to meet together for another three to five sessions to explore their fears of flying in more depth. These final sessions can be very useful in achieving permanent mastery of flying fears. However, the group leader makes it clear that if the group continues beyond this point, it will no longer be a flying group but a therapy group; also that the group can no longer meet under the auspices of the group organizers.

If sufficient group members elect to continue on this basis, the therapist switches gears completely. He focuses on eliciting and working through personality problems. He works no differently than he would with any psychoanalytically oriented therapy group.

Although this chapter has dealt specifically with the flying phobia, there is no reason, in principle, why similar methods could not be applied to a wide variety of phobic reactions (e.g., fears of cars, ships, elevators, subways, tunnels, bridges, high places, darkness, etc.). The necessary ingredients are: 1) a skilled group therapist, 2) a group of highly motivated people with a common goal, 3) the development of strong, positive morale, 4) the willingness to ventilate phobic fears in a group, and 5) a group decision to enter the phobic situation *as a group,* under the guidance of a leader.

Appendix:
Central Offices of Associations
of Psychologists, Psychiatrists,
and Hypnotherapists

AMERICAN ACADEMY OF PSYCHOTHERAPISTS
1 East Wacker Drive
Chicago, Illinois 60601
   Professional society of psychologists, psychiatrists, anthropologists, clergy, social workers, educators, etc., engaged in the practice of psychotherapy.

AMERICAN BOARD OF PROFESSIONAL PSY-
CHOLOGY, INC.
666 Fifth Avenue
New York, New York 10019
   Certification board which conducts written and oral examinations and awards diplomas to advanced specialists in three professional specialties: clinical psychology, industrial psychology, and counseling psychology.

AMERICAN GROUP PSYCHOTHERAPY ASSOCIA-
TION
1790 Broadway
New York, New York 10025
   Psychologists, psychiatrists, social workers, and others in the mental-health field interested in the practice and theory of group psychotherapy. This is *the* national association of American group therapists.

AMERICAN PSYCHIATRIC ASSOCIATION
1700 Eighteenth Avenue, N.W.
Washington, D.C. 20009
Professional society of psychiatrists who have M.D. degrees. This is *the* national association of American psychiatrists.

AMERICAN PSYCHOANALYTIC ASSOCIATION
1 East 57th Street
New York, New York 10022
Professional society of medical doctors who are psychiatrists and have specialized in psychoanalysis.

AMERICAN PSYCHOLOGICAL ASSOCIATION
1200 Seventeenth Street, N.W.
Washington, D.C. 20036
Scientific and professional society of psychologists and educators. This is *the* national association of American psychologists. (Psychotherapists generally belong to the Division of Clinical Psychology or the Division of Psychotherapy or both.)

AMERICAN SOCIETY OF CLINICAL HYPNOSIS
800 Washington Avenue, S.E.
Minneapolis, Minnesota
Physicians, dentists, and psychologists with a doctoral degree who utilize hypnotic procedure.

COUNCIL OF PSYCHOANALYTIC PSYCHOTHER-APISTS
17 East 96th Street
New York, New York 10028
Psychiatrists, clinical psychologists, and psychiatric social workers who practice psychotherapy.

SOCIETY FOR CLINICAL AND EXPERIMENTAL
HYPNOSIS
353 West 57th Street
New York, New York 10019

Professional society of physicians, dentists, psychologists, and allied professional persons interested in research in hypnosis and its boundary area.

Selected References

Air Transport Association of America. "How to Fly." Washington, D.C.: Air Transport Association of America pamphlet, 1969.

Aronson, Marvin L. "Acting Out in Individual and Group Psychotherapy," *Journal of the Hillside Hospital,* XIII (1964), 43–48.

————. "Organization of Programs of Conjoint Psychotherapy in Mental Hygiene Clinics," *Psychiatric Quarterly* (supplement), XXIX (1965), 299–310.

————. "Patient Selection in Group Therapy," *Voices,* IV (1968), 93–95.

————. "Resistance in Individual and Group Psychotherapy," *American Journal of Psychotherapy,* XXI (1967), 86–95.

————. "Technical Problems in Combined Therapy," *International Journal of Group Psychotherapy,* XIV (1964), 425–430.

Bainbridge, John. *Like a Homesick Angel.* Boston: Houghton Mifflin, 1964.

Balint, Michael. "Friendly Expanses—Horrid Empty Spaces," *The International Journal of Psychoanalysis,* XXXVI (1955), 225–241.

Bernardo, James T. *Aviation and Space in the Modern World.* Rev. ed. New York: E. P. Dutton, 1968.

Blum, Sam. "Group Therapy: A Special Report," *Redbook,* March, 1960.

Bond, Douglas D. *The Love and the Fear of Flying.* New York: International University Press, 1952.

Burke, Ted. "The Group Movement in America," *Town and Country,* June, 1967.

Catlett, George F. "Circadian Dysrhythmia: A Jet Age Malady," *Modern Medicine,* August, 1970.

Fenichel, Otto. *The Psychoanalytic Theory of Neurosis.* New York: Norton, 1945.

Freud, Sigmund. "Analysis of a Phobia in a Five-Year-Old Boy" (1909), *Collected Papers.* III, 149–289. New York: Basic Books, 1959.

————. *The Interpretation of Dreams.* New York: Basic Books, 1959.

Friedman, Paul. "The Phobias," *American Handbook of Psychiatry,* ed. Sylvano Arieti. Vol. I. New York: Basic Books, 1959.

Gatto, Lucio E. "Understanding the Fear of Flying Syndrome: Psychic Aspects of the Problem," *United States Armed Forces Medical Journal,* V (1954), 1093–1116.

Glick, Burton A. "Conditioning Therapy in Phobias," *American Journal of Psychotherapy,* XXIV (1970), 99–101.

Gutheil, Emil A. *The Handbook of Dream Analysis.* New York: Liveright, 1970 (paperback).

Ivey, Evelyn P. "Recent Advances in the Psychiatric Diagnosis and Treatment of Phobias," *American Journal of Psychotherapy,* XII (1963), 35–50.

Kadis, Asya L., Krasner, Jack D., Winick, Charles, and Foulkes, S. H. *A Practicum of Group Psychotherapy.* New York: Hoeber, 1963.

Lazarus, Arnold A. "Group Therapy of Phobic Disorders by Systematic Deconditioning," *Journal of Abnormal and Social Psychology,* LXIII (1961).

MacClean, G. Donald, and Graff, Robert W. "Behavioral Bibliotherapy: A Simple Home Remedy for Fears," *Psychotherapy,* VII (1970), 118–119.

Paul, Louis. "The Suicidal Self," *Psychotherapy,* VII (1970), 177–180.

Perls, Frederick A. *Gestalt Therapy Verbatim*. Lafayette, California: Real People Press, 1969 (paperback).

Perls, Frederick S., Hefferline, Ralph F., and Goodman, Paul. *Gestalt Therapy*. New York: Dell, 1951 (paperback).

Saul, Leon J., and Fleming, Burton A. "A Clinical Note on the Ego Meaning of Certain Dreams of Flying," *Psychoanalytic Quarterly,* IV (1959), 501–504.

Schiff, Barry J. *The Boeing 707*. New York: Arco, 1967 (paperback).

Schleier, Curt. "A Campaign Against Fear," *Air Travel,* May, 1970, pp. A13–18.

Serling, Robert J. *Loud and Clear*. New York: Dell, 1970 (paperback).

Stever, H. Guyford, Haggerty, James J., and the Editors of *Life*. *Flight*. New York: Time, Inc., 1969.

Tipton, Stuart G. "How Safe Is Flying?" Washington, D.C.: Air Transport Association of America pamphlet, 1970.

Wolberg, Lewis R. *The Technique of Psychotherapy*. Vol. II. New York: Grune & Stratton, 1967.

———— (ed.). *Short-Term Psychotherapy*. New York: Grune & Stratton, 1965.

Wolf, Alexander. "Short-Term Group Psychotherapy," *Short-Term Psychotherapy,* ed. Lewis R. Wolberg. New York: Grune & Stratton, 1965.

————, and Schwartz, Emanuel K. *Psychoanalysis in Groups*. New York: Grune & Stratton, 1962.

Wolpe, Joseph. *The Practice of Behavior Therapy*. New York: Elmsford, 1969 (paperback).

World Book Encyclopedia, The. Vol. I. Chicago: Field, 1962.

Zane, Manuel D. "How One Psychiatrist Utilizes His Tape Recorder with Patients," *Frontiers of Clinical Psychiatry,* December, 1969.

Index